kitchens
DESIGNS FOR LIVING

Meredith® BOOKS

KITCHENS DESIGNS FOR LIVING®

Contributing Editor: Catherine M. Staub, Lexicon
    Consulting, Inc.
Contributing Associate Editor: Julie Collins, Lexicon
    Consulting, Inc.
Contributing Writer: Martin Miller
Contributing Assistants: Randall Noblet, Holly Reynolds,
    Emma Sarran, Lexicon Consulting, Inc.
Contributing Graphic Designer: On-Purpos, Inc.
Copy Chief: Terri Fredrickson
Publishing Operations Manager: Karen Schirm
Senior Editor, Asset and Information Manager: Phillip Morgan
Edit and Design Coordinator: Mary Lee Gavin
Editorial and Design Assistant: Renee E. McAtee
Book Production Managers: Pam Kvitne, Marjorie J.
    Schenkelberg, Rick von Holdt, Mark Weaver
Contributing Copy Editor: Arianna McKinney
Contributing Proofreaders: Julie Cahalan, Becky Danley,
    Dan Degen
Contributing Indexer: Stephanie Reymann
Contributing Photography: Abramowitz Creative Studios
    Lead Photographer: Tim Abramowitz
    Set Production: Tim Arens
    Stylist: Elizabeth Saunders

Meredith® Books

Executive Director, Editorial: Gregory H. Kayko
Executive Director, Design: Matt Strelecki
Managing Editor: Amy Tincher-Durik
Executive Editor/Group Manager: Benjamin W. Allen
Senior Associate Design Director: Tom Wegner
Marketing Product Manager: Brent Wiersma
National Marketing Manager-Home Depot: Suzy Johnson

Publisher and Editor in Chief: James D. Blume
Editorial Director: Linda Raglan Cunningham
Executive Director, Marketing: Steve Malone
Executive Director, New Business Development: Todd M. Davis
Director, Sales-Home Depot: Robb Morris
Executive Director, Sales: Ken Zagor
Director, Operations: George A. Susral
Director, Production: Douglas M. Johnston
Director, Marketing: Amy Nichols
Business Director: Jim Leonard

Vice President and General Manager: Douglas J. Guendel

Meredith Publishing Group
President: Jack Griffin
Senior Vice President: Bob Mate

Meredith Corporation
Chairman and Chief Executive Officer: William T. Kerr
President and Chief Operating Officer: Stephen M. Lacy

In Memoriam: E.T. Meredith III (1933–2003)

The Home Depot®
Marketing Manager: Tom Sattler
© Copyright 2006 by Homer TLC, Inc.
First Edition, Fifth Printing.
All rights reserved.
Printed in the United States of America.
Library of Congress Control Number: 2006921275
ISBN-13: 978-0-696-22879-7
ISBN-10: 0-696-22879-3
The Home Depot® is a registered trademark of
    Homer TLC, Inc.

Distributed by Meredith Corporation.
Meredith Corporation is not affiliated with The Home Depot®.

Note to the Reader: Due to differing conditions, tools
and individual skills, Meredith Corporation and The Home
Depot® assume no responsibility for any damages, injuries
suffered, or losses incurred as a result of attempting to
replicate any of the home improvement ideas portrayed or
otherwise following any of the information published in this
book. Before beginning any project, including any home
improvement project, review the instructions carefully
and thoroughly to ensure that you or your contractor,
if applicable, can properly complete the project, and, if
any doubts or questions remain, consult local experts or
authorities. Because codes and regulations vary greatly,
you should always check with authorities to ensure that
your project complies with all applicable local codes
and regulations. Always read and observe all of the
safety precautions provided by any tool or equipment
manufacturer, and follow all accepted safety procedures.

We are dedicated to providing inspiring, accurate, and
helpful do-it-yourself information. We welcome your
comments about improving this book and ideas for other
books we might offer to home improvement enthusiasts.
Contact us by any of these methods:
Write to:
    Meredith Books, Home Depot Books
    1716 Locust St.
    Des Moines, IA 50309–3023
Send e-mail to: hi123@mdp.com.

contents

how to use this book

Improving your kitchen is an investment in the equity of your home and your quality of life, as well as a reflection of your style and taste. Remodeling and updating an existing kitchen or building a new one can be one of the largest single investments that you will make. The first step in making your dream kitchen a reality is finding a source of inspiration.

That's why the designers and associates at The Home Depot® have put together a collection of attractive and functional kitchen designs in one easy-to-use book. *Kitchens Designs for Living* will inspire you with hundreds of photos and ideas to create an ideal kitchen for your home and your lifestyle.

Whether you intend to design all or part of the kitchen yourself or plan to use the services of an architect or designer, you'll need a resource for ideas and some good advice on the latest possibilities for kitchen designs and styles.

STYLE–FUNCTION–DETAILS. A kitchen layout that works as well as you need it to is more than a floor plan and an appliance order; it's a comprehensive design that will turn your dream into reality. A good kitchen concept is a combination of style, function, and details. It's the result of defining your personal style and taste, considering how you and your family want to use the kitchen now and in the future, and remembering the fine elements that will make the space complete.

Style. The style of your kitchen is a top priority. A decorating scheme can begin with a specific color, texture, or theme you want in your kitchen. With the style in place, decisions about cabinetry, finishes, appliances, fixtures, and countertops will be easier. How much time and effort is put into this phase will ultimately define how happy you'll be in your new kitchen.

Function. The design of your kitchen will fail if its components aren't functional, no matter how much you love the overall style. Consider the purpose of each element in the kitchen—cabinetry, appliances, countertops, floor, lighting, and fixtures—and whether it aids or hinders the function of your kitchen. Remember to design for each member of your family, taking small hands and a limited reach into consideration.

Details. To get exactly what you want, plan for the finishing touches. The style, colors, shapes, and finishes of each element in the room contribute to a pleasing result for the overall room. Things you might consider small details—textures, trim, and window treatments, for example— will finish off the room in fine style. It's the purposeful combination of these elements that creates a kitchen that's unified—yet uniquely yours.

ideas

Creating your ideal kitchen begins with a list of your wants and needs. Beyond your wish list, however, glean ideas from other kitchens to create the perfect space in which to share time with family and friends. To get started, look through this collection of kitchens that blend function and style.

CASUAL DINING (ABOVE) For snacking or quick meals, options besides the dining room table are handy. An extended countertop peninsula with chairs allows casual dining in the kitchen and makes it easy for family to interact with the person preparing the food.

useful elegance

HARD WORK. Your kitchen can look fresh despite daily use if you select materials that stand up to the wear and tear of regular activity and look elegant while doing so. Consider installing quartz countertops, such as those in this kitchen. This durable surface is mostly scratch-resistant, stain-resistant, and scorch-resistant. With any quartz or natural stone surface remember to use trivets for hot items. Quartz is low maintenance so you don't have to sacrifice a clean counter because of a busy schedule. Sealing is not required and it's easy to clean with soap and water.

EASY ON THE EYES. Maintain elegance by using one main color. In this kitchen, for example, amaretto creme-glazed maple cabinets match the white sink and pantry, while other elements, such as the colored quartz countertop, add accent colors.

Stainless-steel appliances, such as this kitchen's range, dishwasher, and refrigerator, evoke a sophisticated feel that continues with the understated shapes of the streamlined vent hood.

GO FOR STRENGTH (LEFT)
Quartz countertops are ideal for hardworking kitchens. Dropped knives won't scratch them, moderate heat won't mar them, and spilled wine or olive oil won't stain them.

BACK TO CLASSICS While modern stainless-steel sinks are popular, this kitchen is well served by a more classic look. An apron-front, undercounter sink is functional and provides a historical presence.

STAY ORGANIZED (ABOVE) This kitchen cabinet features a built-in space on the side with specific spots for keys, mail, pens, and other everyday objects. A whiteboard on the inside of the cabinet door provides a place for messages without taking up extra space on the kitchen wall.

A SMART SOLUTION (BELOW) The position of this microwave oven makes it easy for kids to access it. The countertop provides landing space for hot dishes.

BREAK BOUNDARIES

(LEFT) Cabinet manufacturers often offer fittings that blend vents with the rest of the cabinetry. Here, the wooden range hood keeps with the organic look of the rest of the space.

SMART STORAGE

(RIGHT) Storing cookie sheets and cake pans in a drawer is an alternative to vertical cabinet dividers. Here they're easily accessible for the cook.

SMOOTH TRANSITIONS A small room that opens to the kitchen, such as this home office, looks best when the colors and materials match the kitchen. The wall paint, cabinetry, and flooring in this office helps unify the two rooms.

down to earth

NATURALLY. Going organic isn't limited to food. You can design a natural, earthy kitchen as well. This kitchen features grass-green color on the walls and warm wood tones that evoke a traditional yet comfortable style.

MAPLE AND STEEL. Maple wood with a coffee-color finish is used throughout this kitchen and the adjoining home office, effectively connecting the spaces. Glass inserts in some cabinet doors and an open wine shelf break up expanses of cabinetry. Engineered maple wood flooring with a mahogany glaze offers a rich contrast to the midtone cabinetry.

The stainless-steel refrigerator, oven, and microwave, as well as a stainless-steel backsplash behind the range, provide a pleasing contemporary contrast to the traditional materials in the kitchen.

SAVE THE SPACE (LEFT)
Spice racks integrated with a larger cabinet save space and make it easy to reach items when they are needed. This type of cabinet insert also frees counters from potential clutter.

SUBTLE ILLUMINATION Lighting design is most pleasing when the fixtures match the style of the kitchen. In this kitchen the unassuming etched white opal glass mini pendants above the peninsula extend the natural feel of the space.

MIX IT UP (ABOVE) Engineered
wood flooring set on a diagonal
provides visual contrast to the
geometric shapes in the cabinetry.

TWO CABINET STAINS Honey spice and cabernet stains—applied to the same style of birch cabinetry—create contrast in this kitchen within an overall unified design.

A BIT OF FLASH (RIGHT) Along with accent colors and treatments, simple details such as glass inserts offer personality to the kitchen cabinetry. This decorative glass insert allows the bright colors of the dishes to show.

behind closed doors

COLORFUL DESIGN. Galley kitchens are one of the most efficient kitchen layouts, and with careful planning they offer plenty of space. This kitchen boasts both personality and convenience in a narrow footprint. Birch cabinets with two stains—honey spice for the wall cabinet doors and cabernet for the base cabinets and wall-cabinet frames—create a striking palette when partnered with fresh green walls and black appliances.

CABINETRY FEATURES. To keep countertops clutter-free, this stylish cabinetry offers more than good looks. Fully extendable drawers are deep to house pots and pans right next to the range. One drawer features slotted knife storage topped by a slide-out cutting board. Slotted plate racks built into the cabinetry in lieu of more standard wall cabinets visually open the room—and the display plates provide welcome color.

FIND IT (RIGHT) Dividers in a large-utensil drawer minimize clutter and misplaced items. The organizer in this drawer makes it easy for the cook to find a ladle or ice cream scoop in no time.

MATCH YOUR ACCENTS In a simple kitchen with natural tones, small accents go a long way. For continuity the window treatment, soap dispenser, and blender all are red, pulling in one of the colors found in the dishware.

NATURALLY STYLISH (BELOW) The quartz countertop in this kitchen boasts sophistication and complements the clean-lined cabinets and appliances. It's also a good choice because its surface is nonporous and nearly maintenance-free.

SILVERWARE STORAGE
(ABOVE) Built-in silverware dividers
eliminate the need for add-on
plastic or wire separators in the
functional drawer.

smart planning

HARDWORKING FEATURES. Getting
the most from a modest-size kitchen is
possible with strategic design. This kitchen
is functional thanks to a compact work
area and cabinetry that includes a bounty
of convenient features. The upper and
lower cabinets conceal a trash can, lazy
Susan, spice rack, and pullout drawers.
A wine rack above the refrigerator takes
advantage of often overlooked space. Wine
glasses housed beneath upper cabinets
free up space on the shelves for other items.
Laminate, available in a wide selection
of colors and patterns for a low price,
tops the counters. The nonporous surface
reduces the potential for bacteria and
is easily cleaned.

FOOD-FOCUSED AMENITIES. Though
they don't overwhelm the space, the
appliances in this kitchen simplify
food storage and preparation. A 36-inch
side-by-side refrigerator features slide-
out and spillproof shelves, while its
stainless-steel exterior upholds elegance.
The freestanding electric oven also has
a stainless-steel exterior and features an
impressively large interior for cooking
family meals.

METAL LOOKS Stainless-steel appliances lend elegance and professional style to any kitchen, though they require frequent cleanup because they are prone to showing fingerprints. Colors of wood and flooring can change dramatically depending on the lighting, as in this nighttime photograph.

DASH OF VARIETY
The varied heights of
these wall cabinets
create visual interest.

BREAKFAST NOOK
(ABOVE) Common breakfast needs are grouped near each other to make eating in the morning a breeze.

TEXTURED INTEREST (BELOW) The textured glass inserts in some cabinets distort the view slightly so stacked dishware is visible without being on display completely.

COMPACT DESIGN This compact cook center is actually part of a large kitchen divided into several work areas and spaces for casual and formal dining.

VISUAL INTEREST
(BELOW) A variety of
textures combine for
a pleasing look.

UNDER WRAPS
(RIGHT) This tambour
door keeps frequently
used small appliances
close but out of sight.

HOME WORKS (BELOW) A
desk located just outside the
kitchen work center provides
a handy spot for keeping the
phone and doing paperwork.

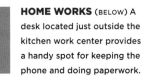

welcome one & all

SMART LAYOUT. This cheery kitchen is designed to function efficiently for a busy family who loves to entertain. The main work zone is a cook-friendly compact area with the storage, prep, cooking, and cleanup areas steps away from each other. Wall ovens are placed just outside the main work area—an ideal spot for less frequently used appliances. The room also features a family organization center with a desk tucked conveniently around the corner from the cooking zone.

ROOM TO ENTERTAIN. If your family loves to entertain, consider opening your kitchen to adjacent areas and include plenty of surfaces for serving spots. This kitchen is separated from the dining room only by a partial wall with a tiled serving ledge. A more casual dining area across from a peninsula eases the transfer of food from cooking to eating spots.

VISUAL INTEREST (ABOVE) Partial walls, columns, and peninsulas divide this open layout into functional areas and make the overall space more visually interesting than one expansive room.

AT YOUR SERVICE (ABOVE) A tile-topped partial wall provides a buffet for the formal dining room that adjoins the kitchen.

BREAK IT UP (BELOW) Narrow glass panels inset into some of the cabinet doors break up what could otherwise be an overwhelming expanse of wood.

LIGHTS PLEASE (ABOVE) Pendent lights are an ideal source of task light in the kitchen. These were installed close enough together so that the resulting pools of light overlap and therefore eliminate shadows.

CONTINUITY IS KEY This kitchen features granite on the countertop, tabletop, and desktop and stainless-steel appliances throughout. The repetition of surface materials provides visual continuity.

COOK WITH STYLE

(LEFT) The cooktop and range hood in this kitchen offer a low-profile design and high-impact style. The glass ceramic cooktop is simple and sleek, and the streamlined range hood with a retractable glass canopy lends modest sophistication.

SOPHISTICATED SINK

(RIGHT) A stainless-steel undercounter sink keeps with the simple and sleek theme of this room, while the extra-large and medium basins provide great workspace.

expansive
surfaces

ILLUMINATING SPACE (ABOVE) These stem-hung miniature pendent lights with swirled alabaster glass are elegant and functional.

GIVE OUT COMPLEMENTS (BELOW) This kitchen features a light beige floor tile that complements the cherry cabinetry. A darker cabinet color, such as mahogany, could be too high contrast with the floor to create a unified space.

STREAMLINED DESIGN. A spacious, sleek, and functional kitchen is easy to achieve. In this kitchen neutral colors and surface repetition are simple design choices that visually expand the space. Extending the use of granite beyond the typical countertop application to the tabletop offers continuity and adds to the expansive feeling.

Stainless-steel appliances further the sophisticated design. The homeowners' choice of a dishwasher with hidden top controls eliminates on-the-door knobs and buttons that could accumulate grime. A cabinet-depth refrigerator maximizes space for easy traffic flow through the kitchen. A compact cooking center—complete with a smooth-surface cooktop and wall ovens with a warming drawer tucked into the far corner of the kitchen—makes it easy for children to remain away from hot surfaces.

rustic yet refined

MAKE IT MANAGEABLE. A large kitchen functions best when it is cordoned off into manageable spaces designed for specific purposes. In this kitchen an island offers a central location for preparing and serving food close to both the cooking and cleanup centers. The sink is flanked by dishwashers to consolidate cleanup activities. Pots and pans suspended above the island are convenient to the range and make an attractive centerpiece for the room.

MATERIAL MIX. This kitchen achieves a pleasing mix of ruggedness and elegance thanks to material choices. The paneled ceiling and knotted wood cabinets partner with more refined countertops and professional-look stainless-steel appliances for a stylish blend.

CREATURE COMFORT
(ABOVE) A fireplace near the eating area offers warmth and comfort.

TAKE A SEAT
(BELOW) Multiple seating areas are conducive for grabbing a snack or a more formal meal.

PLAY THE ANGLES This room takes full advantage of the views with cabinets positioned at angles to follow the wall of bay windows.

 **WORKSPACE** (ABOVE) An island is critical for defining the kitchen area in an open floor plan. It provides an efficient work area for the cook and keeps guests out of the cooking zone.

CLEAN LINES (RIGHT) Long streamlined pulls emphasize the horizontal lines in this kitchen.

**APPLIANCE
FEATURES** (RIGHT)
Many commercial-style
ranges offer additional
features such as a
griddle or grill.

open design

BRING IT TOGETHER. Successful design of an open floor plan depends on a balance between unifying the spaces and defining separate areas. This large area encompasses the kitchen, dining area, and seating area, along with a game table and entertaining spot. Similar neutral colors accented with black and the same large floor tiles throughout the space unify the various functional areas.

SEPARATE AND DEFINE. Several strategies help delineate each functional area within the overall room. An area rug sets off the seating area while a large island at the edge of the kitchen functions as a wall to define the cooking area. A glass-top extension to the island offers informal seating and further emphasizes the more formal role of the dining area. Black support beams visually separate the dining area from the rest of the living room.

fresh country twist

STREAMLINED AND CLEAN. This kitchen exemplifies one approach to current country design, proving a clean, uncluttered look can be achieved along with the warm charm common to country style. Fresh white cabinetry introduces texture with beaded-board panels. Laminated cypress flooring and cinnamon brown walls visually warm the space and add rustic country character.

MULTIPLE COOKS. The kitchen accommodates multiple cooks with multiple work zones. The island includes a prep sink and ample counterspace to prepare food. It is convenient to the main sink and the cooking area but out of the way if another person is cooking or cleaning at the main sink. The refrigerator is positioned slightly outside the main cooking area so children have easy access to snacks without crossing the work zone and getting near hot cooking surfaces.

AT YOUR SERVICE (ABOVE) A built-in bar across from the island functions as a place to serve beverages.

AMPLE ISLAND (RIGHT) An island houses a prep sink and offers plenty of counterspace. The raised counter is ideal for after-school snacks and homework.

COOK ZONE

(RIGHT) The cooking area includes ample counterspace on both sides of the range.

EXTRA NECESSITY
(ABOVE) The large island in this kitchen provides ample space for preparing and serving, a particularly important feature because cooking surfaces, the sink, and other storage limit perimeter counterspace.

DECEIVE WITH DETAIL (LEFT) The trim on the bottom of the maple cabinets is cut to make them appear freestanding, though they are actually typical base cabinets.

PERFECT PLACEMENT (LEFT)
For the cook's convenience this kitchen layout focuses on organization in the drawers and placement within the room. The silverware drawer is positioned smartly near both the range and the island eating area.

COORDINATION AND FUNCTIONALITY (ABOVE)
The brushed nickel faucet in this kitchen complements the dark-tone sink. The large double basin has perks beyond the color: It's ideal for washing large items.

MAKING THE MOST OF IT (BELOW) A downdraft electric cooktop is sleek and useful. The ribbon heating elements provide powerful heat beneath the smooth glass surface, and the bridge element combines three cooktops to create one large cooking area ideal for oversized cooking pans.

in the details

CREATE CHARACTER. Kitchens are about more than cabinets and appliances. Every detail plays a role in creating a successful kitchen design, and this room includes several character-defining elements. With a base of contemporary appliances and simple countertops, varied shapes, colors, and finishes create a kitchen with personality. The fluid shape of the sleek, diamond-quilted opaque glass pendants above the island goes beyond basic lighting and adds simple sophistication to the entire room. The vanilla bean glaze on the maple cabinets is an ideal fit for a refined and upscale country kitchen. The creamy, semitransparent glaze is accented with a warm brown in the corners and profile recesses.

Livability is also important in the kitchen. Cushions on the stools make for comfortable casual seating and serve as decoration. Down to each detail this kitchen exudes a distinct personality.

design

Facing the challenge of where to put everything that belongs in a kitchen—from appliances and cabinets to countertops and lighting—begins with the answer to one question: "What do you want to do in this room?" Once you answer that, begin exploring the possibilities for creating a kitchen layout that best fits your needs and the shape of your space.

CUSTOM KITCHEN
Custom-designed maple cabinets structure this room with bold rectangles and squares. The custom cabinetry ensures every inch of the kitchen is used by providing storage space everywhere from under the island to above the cooktop.

ART EFFECTS (LEFT) Functionality and style go hand in hand in this kitchen that opens up to a banquette and family room. The compact workspace receives boosts of color from cherry cabinets and glass art displayed on shelves.

cooking up a great design

ALL ABOUT YOU. From the moment you begin planning your kitchen, your goal should be to design a space with the largest and most functional work and storage areas possible. At the same time, you want to create a kitchen style that fits you and your home. As much as your layout will be impacted by the size and configuration of the available space, it should also be created with your preferences and lifestyle in mind.

CONSIDER THE BASICS. A kitchen that works well is well organized. Major fixtures and appliances should be easily accessible and logically located in relation to one another. Lighting should illuminate each work area, and the kitchen should be laid out so that traffic moves smoothly. Store utensils close to where you use them. Install ample lighting for all work spaces and design room to move through the kitchen without obstruction. Above all, make sure your kitchen accommodates your lifestyle.

EXTRA, EXTRA (BELOW) This centrally located island is incredibly versatile, providing work and storage space as well as a spot for dining.

FAUCET FIX (ABOVE) A pot-filler faucet on the stove wall adds convenience without intruding on dining or prep space. Such an addition, however, may generate additional plumbing costs.

guidelines

Use basic design standards to define the most efficient and effective kitchen layout.

The National Kitchen and Bath Association (NKBA) developed a set of kitchen design guidelines to plan everything from traffic and work flow to storage and counterspace. The association updates the guidelines periodically to stay current with trends and products. Talk to kitchen designers at The Home Depot for information about efficient and effective kitchen layouts and current guidelines.

ISLAND ESCAPE (ABOVE) Extra leg room under this island countertop allows for stools on three sides, so it's easy for family members to chat while meals are prepared at the island prep sink or on the nearby stove.

ROOM FOR TWO (LEFT) To accommodate two cooks, this large, well-organized kitchen includes two sinks and plenty of counterspace.

RIGHT IDEA (RIGHT)
Ample counterspace
on each side of the
sink makes food prep
and cleanup easy.
This short peninsula
is useful for casual
dining in the kitchen.

kitchen layouts

THE WORK TRIANGLE. At the heart of the most effective kitchen layout lies the work triangle, which efficiently positions the refrigerator, sink, and cooktop or range. A well-designed work triangle reduces the number of steps a cook has to take in meal preparation, cooking, and cleanup and can be applied—with some modifications—to most kitchen layouts.

Typically the triangle should measure no more than 26 feet, although active cooks may prefer 22 feet or less. Each side of the triangle should measure at least 4 feet but no more than 9 feet. These standard measurements may be modified to fit your specific kitchen situation.

SHAPING YOUR SPACE. Kitchen layouts come in a number of shapes and sizes. Depending on the dimensions of your kitchen, one or more of several basic kitchen shapes may work for your space. Keep in mind that the basic shapes are a starting point and possibilities are almost unlimited. You may end up creating a completely original arrangement that works for you.

ADAPTATION (ABOVE) Sheltered under a glass-dome vent, this U-shape preparation area is steps away from food storage and the refrigerator—a modern update of the functional work triangle.

NOT A STRETCH (ABOVE) In this galley kitchen, the refrigerator is located across from the sink and stove. The close proximity of the appliances shows how the work triangle can save steps and energy as the cook travels between the major work stations of the kitchen.

WIDE-OPEN SPACES A barrel-vaulted ceiling arches gracefully over this island-anchored L-shape kitchen. The island works as a visual divider and provides additional storage and prep space.

LAYOUT OPTIONS. For all their variety, most kitchen layouts fit into one of the following categories. You can adjust these basic layouts to meet your needs.

One-wall kitchens are usually small spaces and are not the most efficient for cooks. This layout works best with the sink in the center, flanked by the fridge and cooktop with 4 feet of counter between each. Use apartment-size appliances to increase countertop area.

Galley kitchens are more efficient than single-wall kitchens because they are built between parallel walls, allowing the cook to move easily from one work area to another.

L-shape kitchens include two adjacent walls and work best when the work centers are kept close to the crook of the L. Add an island to increase storage and counter space and provide room for more than one cook.

U-shape kitchens generally involve placing one workstation on each of three walls. To allow for at least 4 feet of workspace in the center of the kitchen, the interior space must be at least 8×8 feet. To make a large U-shape kitchen more efficient, add an island with a sink, cooktop, or prep area.

G-shape kitchens include a peninsula, which serves many of the functions of an island but typically takes up less floor space. The peninsula may include a cooktop or sink, and it can also function as a dining bar or buffet.

Two-cook kitchens can be almost any shape and typically are organized so each cook can work without crossing the other's path.

PERFECT PENINSULA
(ABOVE) This graceful G-shape kitchen features a breakfast bar with a curve that facilitates conversation. Uplights beneath the bar and pendent lights above draw attention to the intriguing focal point.

ONE-WALL WONDER
(BELOW) One-wall kitchens can be cramped, but a multipurpose island provides extra counterspace and visually divides the kitchen from the living area.

A FRESH ANGLE (ABOVE) The addition of a half-wall with a counter transformed this small, unwieldy L-shape kitchen into a stylish and efficient G-shape room. Open storage and glass fronts on some of the cabinets keep the small space from appearing too cramped.

ISLAND MAGIC (RIGHT) The design of this kitchen shows how an island can open up an L-shape layout. Wider than normal walkways keep traffic running smoothly and ensure the island is accessible, even when the dishwasher and oven doors are open.

CREATIVE LAYOUT (LEFT) Rather than following a standard layout, this space gets creative with two island workstations that allow adults to cook at one while kids are doing crafts and homework at the other.

ROOM TO MOVE (BELOW) Where possible, allow at least 42 inches of aisle space on all sides of an island; 48 inches is even better in a two-cook kitchen.

CREATIVE SETUP (RIGHT) This kitchen boasts well-defined work zones built around an island used for food prep and eating. The cooking area includes a cooktop, double oven, and deep sink, while the cleanup zone (*not shown*) on the other side of the island includes a sink and dishwasher.

EASY PREP (BELOW) An island prep sink located close to the stove saves the cook steps in this L-shape kitchen where the main sink is located away from the cooking area.

TEXTBOOK DESIGN (ABOVE) With food storage and the range on one wall and the sink and storage for dishes on the other, this is a classic example of an effective work triangle in a galley kitchen.

EFFICIENT PLAN (LEFT) Considered one of the most efficient and versatile kitchen layouts, this U-shape design situates the cooktop, sink, and refrigerator (*not shown*) on separate walls. However, U shapes can be a tight squeeze for more than one cook if they're in small kitchens such as this one.

SMART ARRANGEMENT
(ABOVE) The oven is often the least used major appliance in the kitchen and may be located just outside the work triangle to gain cabinet space.

HELPFUL EXTENSION (RIGHT) A U-shape kitchen layout with the addition of a peninsula ensures that each task—food prep, cooking, eating, and cleaning—has its own area with plenty of space.

PREP AND CLEAN
(RIGHT) Adding a sink to an island combines preparation and cleanup space in one unit, which is particularly useful in a small kitchen.

work centers

CENTER STAGE. The work center is a kitchen-planning tool that complements the work triangle. By planning separate areas for food preparation, cooking, and cleanup, each of these functions can be carried out as efficiently as possible. Such work centers are particularly useful when more than one cook is in the kitchen—while one cook is preparing food, another can do the cooking or wash dishes nearby.

In addition to the most common work centers, you may also wish to include separate areas for snacks, breakfast, dining, or paying bills. Learn more about specialty centers in the next chapter.

CLOSE AT HAND (LEFT) A work center that includes commonly used tools makes food preparation a smooth operation. Here a section of butcher block with knife slots makes cutting vegetables easy.

SEEING DOUBLE (BELOW) Two sinks really are better than one. A prep sink in the island with a pullout faucet is ideal for food prep, while the long hose on the main sink faucet makes filling large pots easy.

food prep

PARK AND PREPARE. The food preparation center should be fully functional with enough space to prepare everything from large dinners to quick snacks. The most important component of any prep center is counterspace—whether it's located adjacent to the stove, on an island, or on a nearby table. It makes sense to store frequently used items such as knives, spices, and cutting boards near the prep area.

When preparing a meal, you need easy access to a sink for washing vegetables and filling pots with water. A secondary sink and its adjoining counterspace—often located on an island—is ideal for washing and chopping vegetables. Also consider a pot-filler faucet mounted at the cooktop so you don't have to lug large pots of water from sink to cooktop.

Ideally food storage and prep go hand in hand as well. Situating the primary food storage near the longest stretch of countertop makes for easy access to items while cooking.

MOVABLE WORKSPACE (ABOVE)
A movable cart with a butcher-block top is useful for preparing foods close to the stove when there's not room for a full-size island.

STREAMLINED DESIGN (RIGHT) Minimal counterspace need not cramp food preparation activities. This drawer features a slotted knife holder on the bottom with a pullout cutting board on top. Just pull open the drawer when you need additional workspace.

HOT STUFF (ABOVE) Granite is a heat-resistant surface that is ideal as a countertop near a cooktop or range. Cooking tools not located beside the range are conveniently stored within reach in an island, which also adds extra landing space for hot dishes.

CORNER PLAN
(RIGHT) A microwave located on the counter near the cooktop makes quick cooking easy. A peninsula is a convenient spot for a range—the lower level serves as the cooking area, while the upper level forms a backsplash and serving ledge.

COOKING ISLAND (BELOW) A central island with a cooktop and suspended ventilation hood divides the kitchen into cooking and eating areas. Its raised counter conceals clutter from view.

cooking

THE HOT SPOT. Cooking centers are busy stations typically arranged around the cooktop or range. In some homes, a microwave oven may be included in the cooking area, while in others it is used primarily to prepare snacks and is housed in a separate area outside the work triangle. The oven is often situated outside the main work area as well because it is used less frequently.

No matter what appliances comprise your cooking center, incorporate an adequate ventilation system. Where possible, at least 18 inches of counterspace on each side of the cooktop is also recommended for safety and efficiency.

Consider storing commonly used items such as pots and pans, utensils, hot pads, spices, and cooking oils near the cooking zone. If you entertain frequently, you may also wish to include warming drawers nearby.

cleanup

SINK CENTRAL. Because the sink—a key feature of the cleanup center—is called into service for a multitude of kitchen activities, it's best to place the cleanup center between the refrigerator and cooking zone.

Other important components of the cleanup center are the dishwasher, garbage disposal, and trash and recycling containers. The dishwasher should be placed next to the sink—typically it should go on the left of the sink if the main cook is right-handed and to the right if the cook is left-handed. If you entertain often, you may wish to include two dishwashers. Consider placing dishwashers on both sides of the sink, or set one in an island directly across from the main sink. It is also useful to have the trash container close at hand; if you install a trash compactor, place it on the side of the sink opposite the dishwasher.

Also remember to include space for storing dish towels, sponges, and cleaning supplies nearby.

NEXT TO THE SINK
(RIGHT) Installing the dishwasher next to the sink is the most logical location. This extra-deep sink is a boon when it comes to washing deep pots and long baking sheets.

at your **disposal**

Garbage disposal units come in two basic forms—batch feed and continuous. Regardless of which type you choose, be sure to include an electrical outlet in the base cabinet because most models require electricity.

Batch-feed models operate only when the disposal lid is engaged. Continuous models turn on with the flick of a switch and run until you turn the switch off. Although neither type of disposal is completely silent, models with larger cases are often better insulated and quieter. Your best bet is a 1-horsepower unit rather than a $\frac{1}{2}$-horsepower model—more power reduces the likelihood of jamming and means less time at the sink. A sink's style may also affect your disposal choice. An inexpensive stainless-steel sink may not provide solid support for a heavier, high-powered model. Overpowering your sink may cause the unit to rattle the surrounding countertop and cabinets.

A LITTLE THOUGHT
(ABOVE) Making a kitchen more accessible doesn't take a lot of rethinking. Solutions lie in lowered countertops, deeply recessed toe-kicks, and plenty of open floor space.

WITHIN REACH (LEFT) A six-burner cooktop-and-grill unit has easy-grab front knobs and space under the cooktop to make room for a wheelchair. Drawer storage is within arm's reach to the left of the range, while a stainless-steel sink and roll-out waste container are on the right.

accessibility

EASY ACCESS. Accessibility is often taken for granted (or overlooked) when homeowners begin planning a kitchen, but it's something worth considering to ensure your kitchen is easier for all family members and visitors to use regardless of physical ability.

USER-FRIENDLY IDEAS. Here are some modifications that will make your kitchen easier for everyone to use:

- Install drawers with wide pulls rather than knobs and cabinet doors that slide horizontally rather than pivoting outward.
- Plan for a continuous line of countertop absent of any obstructions to allow the cook to slide mixing and cooking vessels from one workstation to another. Also plan for extra countertop space on each side of the cooktop and oven so that hot dishes can be set down.
- Lower sections of the countertop for easy use by seated cooks and leave plenty of knee space underneath to accommodate wheelchair users.
- Place sink faucets toward the front of the sink for easy reach. Use single-control faucets whenever possible.
- Install a side-by-side refrigerator, a cooktop with controls at the front, and a separate oven with a side-opening door.

ON THE LEVEL (ABOVE)
A microwave lowered to chair-level height with supply drawers beneath makes heating food easier.

universal **design**

The term "universal design" often is mistakenly used as a synonym for "accessibility standards." The terms are related but not equivalent.

Universal design is an approach to the design of objects, facilities, and environments aimed at making them easily used by all persons, not just those with physical challenges. Underlying this view is the belief that things and spaces should be usable by people with disabilities in a way that dignifies them. After all, large-print labels are easier to read for everyone, not just the vision impaired, and public telephones that boost the volume make conversation clearer for all people. Universal design supporters promote integrating such improvements into the design from the beginning to avoid the unattractive appearance of accessible afterthoughts.

specialty zones

A kitchen truly is a multifaceted space that reflects your lifestyle and personality as it caters to your specific needs. When you plan your kitchen, be sure to include specialty zones custom-made for your family, whether you want to serve meals right in the kitchen, create a spot for planning menus and paying bills, or include an area for exploring your culinary creativity.

EVERYTHING'S SET
(RIGHT) A small second sink in a snack station eases cleanup. Placing a snack area next to a pantry ensures food is within easy reach.

snack areas

WELCOME SETUP
(ABOVE) A stretch of countertop becomes a snack center when a microwave oven is tucked in a slot between the cabinetry above.

OUT OF THE ACTION (BELOW) A refrigerator next to the table makes it easy to grab and eat snacks without intruding in the cook's work area.

IT'S A TREAT. Creating a separate snack center away from your main food preparation area gives every member of the family easy access to breakfast food or after-school snacks out of the way of the cook. A snack zone may be as simple as a raised section of an island where kids can grab a bite to eat while they work on homework. Or it may be a self-contained countertop area away from the work zone that is just the right size for preparing simple food.

SNACK ATTACK. Placing a microwave in a snack zone offers flexibility for warming up leftovers or cooking microwavable snacks. Include a toaster for making toast, frozen waffles, and other breakfast foods. If your snack zone is not located near a full-size refrigerator, consider installing a refrigerator drawer for storing juices, milk, and refrigerated snack foods. Be sure to include storage close by for breads, health bars, cereals, and other snacks, as well as space for storing plastic cups, dishes, silverware, and napkins.

EASY REACH (LEFT)
A microwave tucked in a niche on the island is accessible from either side, so kids sitting at the counter can heat up a snack well away from a hot range while cooks can use it for quick cooking. An outlet next to the microwave facilitates the use of extra appliances such as a toaster.

SMART SEPARATION An expansive island seems less so with a divider that separates food prep and eating areas. The short wall hides countertop clutter while keeping the view open, and cutouts in the divider serve as storage and display nooks.

LOFT SOLUTIONS (LEFT) A two-tier peninsula creates a U-shape kitchen work area as well as a spot for dining in a loft apartment.

eat-in kitchens

SMALL SPACES, BIG SOLUTIONS. Even if space is tight in your kitchen, consider including an area for informal dining. These spots are ideal for snack time, family meals, and casual get-togethers.

Dining close to the core of the kitchen encourages interaction between the person who is cooking and other family members or guests. Plus an eating area close to the cooking zone makes serving meals and clearing away dishes easy.

BOOTHS AND BANQUETTES. Allow for extra floor space if you want to include a table with chairs in your kitchen. Round tables fit better into small spaces than square or rectangular ones.

An island or peninsula with room for stools or tall chairs takes up less room and provides added workspace for the cook as well as a buffet-style serving area for parties. These types of eat-in accommodations also make nice transitional elements in open kitchen designs and visually separate the kitchen from adjacent rooms.

If you have a spare corner or a spot in front of a window, consider installing a booth or banquette. These mini dining rooms make great spaces for enjoying morning coffee or cozy meals close to the action but out of the food prep and cooking zones.

VERSATILE EXTENSION (BELOW) Even a short peninsula can be used as a snacktime space. It's the perfect spot for making a batch of popcorn or other snacks without moving the mess into the adjacent family room.

TABLE FOR TWO This lava-stone island countertop provides the perfect spot for eating opposite the cooktop. Many islands are topped with different materials than the counters found elsewhere in the kitchen.

HOMESTYLE EATING (BELOW) This old-fashioned farmhouse-style table takes the place of an island in the middle of a large kitchen. The table, surrounded by stools instead of chairs, gives family members and guests a place to gather without hindering cooking activities.

DINING IN THE SUN (RIGHT) This kitchen takes advantage of natural light by positioning a banquette in front of a large window in the kitchen. A nearby countertop facilitates serving food to guests who are already seated.

DOUBLE DUTY

(LEFT) A banquette with additional storage beneath the seat makes use of extra space in a tight kitchen. It's a great spot to stash appliances that aren't used often.

PERFECT SETTING

(ABOVE) This tiny corner breakfast nook looks particularly inviting thanks to cheerful striped seat cushions and a funky wrought-iron and glass table topped with fresh flowers.

QUAINT CORNER

(BELOW) This small table may not be large enough for full-scale meals, but it's the perfect size for intimate family breakfasts. Ample natural light creates a welcoming setting just after sunrise.

breakfast nooks

FOR MORNING OR EVENING. Despite the name, breakfast nooks are not reserved solely for morning use. They're actually a variation on the traditional eat-in kitchen that allows family to gather casually around a table that's away from the kitchen work core but not in a separate formal dining room.

Breakfast nooks come in a variety of shapes, sizes, and styles. Whether they feature a round or square table and built-in bench seating or freestanding chairs depends on the space and your personal preference. Decorate your breakfast nook to match the nearby kitchen or give it a style all its own. These spaces almost always include windows—it's the sunny natural light that makes them so appealing at breakfast time. Often a single light overhead—such as a pendent fixture or small chandelier—ensures that a breakfast nook is inviting on overcast days and even after dark.

WINDOW SEATS

Two benches make use
of this space beneath
a corner window. The
round table prevents
bumps and bruises from
sharp corners and slides
out so those who choose
bench seats can enter
and exit gracefully.

PLENTY OF EVERYTHING

(BELOW) A baking center for making perfect pastry includes plenty of storage space for dry ingredients and utensils. A marble countertop is ideal for rolling and kneading dough.

DEDICATED GARAGE (RIGHT)

This appliance garage devoted to baking tools is easily accessible thanks to scissor hinges. Heavy items such as this mixer can be plugged into an outlet hidden in the garage and pulled forward for immediate use rather than lugged elsewhere in the kitchen.

baking centers

BETTER BAKING. If baking is your specialty—or even just a favorite way to spend time in the kitchen—consider including a baking center. This area might be a corner of the kitchen with plenty of open counterspace and cabinetry stocked with baking supplies. Or it might be an area outside the main work core near a wall oven—or even in an adjacent butler's pantry—outfitted with the necessary supplies.

Typically baking requires the use of small appliances such as a mixer or bread machine, so make certain at least one electrical outlet is located in the baking center area. In addition storage is a must for tools including mixing bowls, baking pans, cookie sheets, and utensils. It makes sense to keep ingredients that are used often—particularly flour, sugar, and spices—close at hand too.

SWEET SPOT (ABOVE) In this compact kitchen, a lowered countertop surface near a window provides a pleasant spot for baking prep and makes rolling and mixing easier. Cupboards under the counter are perfect for stashing mixing bowls and cookie sheets.

EASY INDULGENCE (ABOVE) All that's
required to brew espresso for guests is space
on the counter near an electrical outlet—and
this kitchen has plenty. A location near coffee
cups, saucers, and silverware is also a plus.

coffee nooks

EYE-OPENERS. If you're the type of person who has to grab a cup of coffee before the day officially begins, a coffee center is a worthwhile kitchen addition.

Perhaps you can get by with a bit of counterspace for a standard coffeemaker near the cupboard where you store your mugs. A freestanding coffeemaker typically requires little more than an electrical outlet, although you may wish to place it close to a sink so you don't have to haul water across the kitchen.

Then again, you could go all out with a built-in coffee unit that includes an espresso maker. Such a unit requires a dedicated water line, so plan accordingly. With such a setup, you'll probably want to include storage space nearby to house a coffee bean grinder and an assortment of coffees and sugars.

Depending on where your built-in coffee center is located, consider combining it with a toaster, bins of cereal, and other breakfast items as well.

GOOD MORNING (ABOVE)
A pullout shelf serves as a handy perch for pastries and coffee cups below a built-in coffee center.

HOT COFFEE (ABOVE)
A microwave oven near a coffeemaker provides a spot for reheating beverages that have cooled off.

MORNING APPLIANCES (RIGHT)
When not in use, the equipment for morning coffee is hidden behind this tambour door.

TIGHT SQUEEZE
This small desk area fits perfectly next to a pantry and broom closet. Mail slots above the desk create a vintage feel and corral small objects.

A NATURAL EXTENSION (RIGHT)
The same cabinets, hardware, countertops, and backsplash unite this organization center and kitchen.

organization centers

THE PLANNING SPOT. This incredibly functional kitchen space is the spot where family members write letters, pay bills, plan menus, or do homework. Putting a workspace in or near the kitchen sets it close to the center of family activities so it's available to everyone and allows easy monitoring of computer activity. Employ the same style and cabinetry in this area as you have in the kitchen to create an integrated design.

ORGANIZING YOUR SPACE. At a minimum include a desk or work surface, a chair, and a filing drawer at your organization center. Beyond the basics, if you choose to include a computer, telephone, and lamp, be sure to install the necessary electrical outlets and proper phone and computer connections.

Take stock of all the items—including paper, stamps, folders, stationery, markers, and so on—that you might use in this space so you can plan proper storage in the surrounding cabinets and drawers. You may also want to hang a chalkboard or bulletin board nearby to keep track of family activities.

JUST A NOTE
(RIGHT) A blackboard from an office supply outlet cut to size makes a centrally located family communication center in this kitchen.

HOME OFFICE (ABOVE) Angled at one end of the room, this home office has plenty of drawers, cabinets, and cubbyholes for storing financial records and school supplies. Cabinets located in a kitchen office may contain extra kitchen items such as seldom-used seasonal dishes as well.

EFFICIENT MESSENGER (RIGHT) A message center with a cork-backed door keeps a busy family organized and provides a place to hold the phone, sort the mail, and store papers.

IN THE CORNER
A lowered counter sets a desk area off from the adjacent kitchen cabinets and counter. The window in front of it makes the tight corner seem almost spacious. Nearby, a curved granite countertop offers front-row kitchen seating when homework is finished.

PRIME LOCATION
(ABOVE) These cabinets keep all the stemware in one place to save steps and make serving beverages easier.

CLEAN LINES, CLEANUP
(LEFT) Designed with unobtrusive contemporary lines, this entertaining area includes a bar sink, wine cooler, and undercounter refrigerator perfect for party prep and cleanup.

entertaining

PARTY RIGHT. For some reason guests tend to congregate in the kitchen during parties or family gatherings, which often means they're right in the food prep and cooking zones. If you entertain often, you may want to create space outside the cooking zone and outfit it with everything needed to make throwing a party stress-free and thoroughly enjoyable.

SMOOTH TRANSITION. Ultimately your goal is to provide a space for guests to mingle close to the action in the kitchen but out of the way of the person doing the cooking. This may be an extension of the kitchen cabinetry and countertop that is beyond the work triangle, or it may be a separate area just outside of the kitchen.

This entertainment setup may be as simple as a cabinet for glasses and a length of countertop large enough for mixing drinks and serving appetizers. If you entertain frequently, you may wish to include an undercounter refrigerator for stashing beverages and a prep sink for washing glasses. Other amenities that come in handy for frequent entertaining include an icemaker, microwave, and wine refrigerator.

READY TO PARTY (RIGHT) Frosted glass inserts hint at what hides behind these stainless-steel upper cabinets. Amenities include a bar sink, dishwasher drawer, and undercounter refrigerator.

EASY DOES IT (RIGHT) A bar area doesn't have to be fancy—this one has the basics covered with storage for glasses, wine bottles, and cold beverages so guests can get their own drinks.

SINGULAR STYLE
The same wood tones unify this dining table and chairs with the kitchen cabinetry.

CASUAL ATTITUDE (LEFT)
It's natural for a kitchen to flow into a living area such as this one. A consistent color scheme combined with uniform flooring and lighting unites the two spaces and makes it easier for people to move between the rooms.

adjacent rooms

GO WITH THE FLOW. In the past most rooms in a house were conceived as separate entities with little or no relationship to the rest of the home. Today open design highlights and encourages connections between rooms, creating a more unified design without sacrificing the identity of each space.

It makes sense to have the kitchen—the hub of many busy homes—open and accessible to surrounding rooms. While dinner is being prepared, kids might be playing steps away in the living room. For serving large family meals, it's convenient to have the dining room right next door. And large-scale entertaining often requires more storage and preparation space than the kitchen allows, so why not include a butler's pantry nearby?

UNIFYING ELEMENTS. Although each space retains its unique identity, rooms that open to one another should incorporate some unifying—or at least complementary—design elements. Install the same flooring in two rooms to visually combine the spaces, or use different materials or patterns to distinguish one area from another. The same holds true for ceiling heights, lighting, and even the selection of furnishings and decor.

BUTLER'S PANTRY

(ABOVE) Fitted with cabinetry to match the kitchen, a butler's pantry becomes a staging area for meals served in an adjacent formal dining room as well as a spot for storing glassware.

FORMAL ATTIRE (ABOVE) Although the white cabinetry in the dining room sets it apart from the darker wood tones found in the adjacent kitchen, having the rooms open to one another facilitates serving meals and clearing away dishes.

EASY TO REACH (ABOVE) Situated just outside the main cooking area, this narrow pantry provides storage for items not needed on an everyday basis.

NATURAL CONNECTION (RIGHT) Sunny days are far too precious to keep the busiest room of the house cut off from the outdoors. Opening the kitchen to the backyard is particularly useful for summertime alfresco entertaining.

BLUE AND WHITE
White columns separate the kitchen from a small dining area, which serves as an extension of the cooking space while retaining its distinct identity. Blue and white details unite the areas.

cabinetry

Nothing sets the look and feel of your kitchen quite like cabinetry. Aside from establishing the style of your space, cabinets are pivotal for creating a kitchen that's efficient and easy to use. Considering all the items used in an average kitchen, you need space for nearly 800 objects. Cabinets take care of almost all of them neatly.

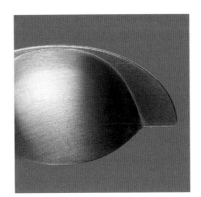

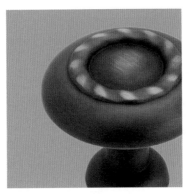

EASY DISPLAY (ABOVE) Standard cabinets don't have to look boring. Glass inserts in select upper cabinets lend visual variety and are perfect for displaying glassware and dishes.

JUST FOR YOU (BELOW) Custom cabinetry featuring everything from open shelving and apothecary drawers to tambour doors and niches for appliances fits this kitchen's storage needs and style.

cabinetry basics

NOT SO STANDARD. On one level, categorizing cabinetry is easy—every piece is either a wall cabinet, which is hung on the wall, or a base cabinet, which sits on the floor. If every wall or base cabinet came in one standard style, however, they'd never meet the varied needs each kitchen owner faces.

Fortunately both wall and base cabinets come in a number of configurations—with doors, with drawers, with doors and drawers, single units, double units, corner units. The list goes on. Specialty cabinets house refrigerators, cooktops, and other appliances. Other units run from floor to ceiling or fit beneath island countertops—you get the idea.

GET SOME GUIDANCE. Jumpstart your cabinet planning by assessing your needs and what you have to store in your kitchen. First consider what cabinets are needed for each work center; then fill in the spaces left with other units. Make a list of everything you store in your kitchen so you can choose cabinet sizes, drawers, and shelves based on what will go inside each unit. Survey what's available for pullouts and accessories to make organizing your kitchen easier. (For more kitchen storage information, turn to page 172.)

PERFECTLY UNFITTED (ABOVE) Semicustom
cabinetry mixes with buffets, bookshelves, and
other furnishings obtained from antiques shops and
auctions. The variety of materials, textures, and colors
creates a style that's impossible to duplicate with
standard cabinetry.

HIGH STYLE (ABOVE) High-end cabinetry is worthy of its price tag for its appearance, long-lasting quality, and precision construction, as the detailing on this built-in hutch illustrates.

LOVELY DISPLAY (LEFT) A long bank of yellow cabinets with glass inserts displays china. The countertop works well as a buffet serving space.

cabinet **construction**

Cabinets fall into three basic categories—stock, semicustom, and custom—depending on how they're constructed and whether they can be customized.

▸ **STOCK CABINETS,** the least expensive option, come in standard sizes and styles. The units arrive at your home either fully assembled or ready to assemble. Stock cabinet finishes and quality can be quite good, but they don't come in special sizes and accessories are limited.

▸ **SEMICUSTOM CABINETS** are built with better materials and more design flexibility. Modifications to standard cabinet sizes can be made and the addition of storage units and accessories is possible. Be prepared to pay more for semicustom cabinets and wait longer for your order than you would with stock models.

▸ **CUSTOM CABINETS** are built by a cabinetmaker from the material you choose in the size, shape, configuration, and finish you specify so your cabinets look and function just as you want them to. Remember that custom cabinets are expensive, and they may take 10 weeks to complete.

TALL ORDER (RIGHT)
Cabinetry extended
to the ceiling creates
both a sleek, modern
impression and storage
space. Glass inserts
lighten the expanse of
dark wood cabinetry.

PICTURE PERFECT (ABOVE)
Rustic old-world cabinets with fluted corner columns pair with painted cabinetry along the perimeter of this kitchen. The painted cabinets act as a frame for the focal-point cooking center and island.

cabinet styles

MAKING AN APPEARANCE. You've heard it before, and you'll hear it again. Cabinets greatly influence the style of your kitchen. Consider what look you're after and select cabinets accordingly. Common styles are defined in a large part by the style of the cabinet doors.

Traditional cabinetry offers a timeless look with wood doors that include raised panels and ornate molding.

Country cabinetry is a bit more casual with fewer ornate details. These wood cabinets typically feature recessed or raised door panels.

Shaker cabinetry offers a traditional look with frame-and-recessed-panel doors that add dimension.

Arts and Crafts cabinetry is casual too, with inset flat panel doors and occasional glass inserts for showing off what's stored inside.

Contemporary cabinetry makes a statement, often with flat-panel doors and a laminate finish in colors such as white or black.

CLEAN AND CONTEMPORARY (BELOW) This streamlined kitchen includes the sleek, clean lines of frameless cabinetry. The toe-kicks were removed and legs fashioned from plumbing hardware capped with protective rubber tips were installed.

EUROPEAN STYLE Painted French blue with a distressed finish, the English-style cabinetry in this kitchen includes handcrafted pieces outfitted with period details. The result is a decidedly unfitted appearance.

fitted or **unfitted?**

Whether you choose fitted or unfitted cabinetry depends on personal preference.

Fitted cabinetry typically features banks of matching base and wall cabinets, an option that allows for optimum storage and counterspace. Cabinet styles in a fitted kitchen range from contemporary to traditional. To spice up this style put specialty glass inserts in some cabinets and add detailing such as corbels.

An unfitted kitchen features freestanding, unmatched furniturelike cabinetry. These units bring flexibility to your kitchen design and make it easier to create a style that looks as if it has evolved over time.

SHELVES FOR SHOW (LEFT) This end unit's light-stained finish makes the perfect background for showing off colorful glassware.

EASY AND VINTAGE (BELOW) Simple cabinets with inset doors and beaded-board edging convey vintage style. The putty color of the cabinets was chosen for its historical correctness and ease of maintenance.

RETRO FIT (BELOW) Blue drawer fronts and pale yellow frames combine with black-and-white backsplash tiles for a breezy retro-cottage look. Pebbled glass door inserts make the wall cabinets appear light and open.

SHELF LIFE (RIGHT)
Open shelving provides storage in a kitchen with ceilings too low for wall cabinets. Small track lights help draw attention to items above eye level.

door **styles**

Doors and drawers constitute the face of cabinetry and have a major impact on the appearance of your kitchen. They come in several styles.

▸ **SLAB DOORS,** typically made in one piece from laminate woods, present a smooth exterior surface and are the style most often found on frameless cabinets.

▸ **RAISED-PANEL DOORS** feature a panel milled with a raised appearance.

▸ **RECESSED-PANEL DOORS** contain inset center panels that may have simple profiles or more elaborate treatments.

▸ **GLASS-PANEL DOORS** have a frame that houses a pane of glass. Inset glass styles may be clear, colored, ribbed, or frosted— each style creates a different effect.

Aside from cabinet door style, consider how the door fits over the cabinet box. Doors may be partial overlay, full overlay, flush inset, or lipped.

OUTSIDE THE BOX (ABOVE) Not all kitchen elements have to be contained within the cooking area. This cherry hutch located just outside the kitchen stores less frequently used table linens and glassware.

STREAMLINED SPOT
Contemporary style
is characterized by its
uncluttered look and use
of industrial materials.
Hardware-free frameless
cabinets constructed of a
gloss-free laminate occupy
the lower half of this kitchen.
Windows take the place of
upper cabinets to further the
streamlined look.

UP THE LADDER

(RIGHT) A gliding library ladder provides access to high-level storage. See-through doors with beveled glass inserts lighten the look of an entire wall of floor-to-ceiling cabinets.

NOW YOU SEE IT

(BELOW) Color and special effects, such as this textured glass insert, play a major role in cabinet selection. Textured glass is ideal for creating a sense of mystery while still providing a glimpse of what's inside.

doors & drawers

CUSTOM CHOICES. Determining where to install cabinets and where to use drawers is a matter of personal preference. Standard kitchen setups involve upper and lower cabinets with a row of drawers situated directly below the countertop. Custom cabinetry is so common now, however, that you can expand on this organization.

PUSH AND PULL. As a general rule, cabinets are outfitted with shelves, making them a versatile option for storing everything from glassware and mixing bowls to small appliances and boxes of dry goods. Drawers, which are typically narrower and shallower than cabinets, are most often used for storing smaller objects such as silverware and cooking utensils. New cabinetry options are blurring the lines between doors and drawers, however. It's becoming more common for kitchens to include heavy-duty objects such as pots and pans in drawers. On the other hand if you like the traditional appearance of cabinet doors but want the functionality of drawers, pullout shelves offer the best of both worlds.

AGELESS EFFECT (ABOVE) Raised-panel doors and drawers establish traditional style. Dark wrought-iron handles and knobs stand out against the white cabinetry.

BASKET CASE To break up a bank of cabinetry and add textural variety to an island, include a row or two of baskets. They corral items and pull out much as drawers do.

COLORFUL DISPLAY (RIGHT) Narrow vertical slots at the front of these island storage bins display an assortment of dried beans, pasta, and popcorn. Drawer space behind the display slots is used for storing dry goods.

NO HANDLES (RIGHT) Eurostyle drawers can be handle-free. These drawers feature a recess in the front edge, providing finger pulls for opening.

HEAVY LOAD (LEFT) Some base cabinet drawers now are designed to hold heavy pots and pans. Full-extension hardware allows the drawer to open completely in order to access items in the back.

indications **of quality**

Take a look at the construction of drawers to gauge cabinet quality before you make a purchase.

Begin by testing the drawer to see how smoothly and quietly it moves in and out. Then look at the construction of the drawer. It should have $1/2$- or $3/4$-inch solid wood sides and a $3/16$- or $1/4$-inch plywood bottom set in a groove on all four sides. Thinner plywood may bow under the weight of drawer contents. Dovetailed joints are an indication of quality drawer construction, but high-quality glides account for most of the difference between an average drawer and one that's superior. Full-extension glides allow full access to the drawer and should have stops and bumpers to keep drawers from falling out. Self-closing drawers are also a desirable feature. They close by themselves when within an inch of the opening.

COLOR ME BEAUTIFUL (ABOVE)
The vivid purpleheart wood of this drawer looks particularly striking when paired with the light tones of classic maple.

TWO TONES (LEFT)
With one finish for the cabinet box and a contrasting finish for the doors, this cabinetry proves that standard storage doesn't have to be boring.

materials
& finishes

UNDER COVER. Cabinet materials affect how the units look and how well they stand up to daily use.

Particleboard is a common base material for stock cabinet cases, especially those covered with laminates and vinyl finishes. Midpriced lines are often constructed of a stronger substrate called *medium-density fiberboard* (MDF). For long-lasting, durable cabinetry, look for units made with *heavy-gauge plywood* cases.

Cabinets are typically finished with either *laminates* or *veneers*. A laminate surface is made of three resin-saturated layers fused to the cabinet substrate with heat and pressure. Choices in quality, color, and pattern vary widely. Common options include high-pressure laminates, low-pressure laminates, resin-impregnated or heat-stamped transfer foils, and thermofoil. Wood veneer—thin wood layers sliced from trees—is adhered to plywood or particleboard and treated with a variety of stains, varnishes, and other finishes. When selecting wood veneer, assess the grain, pattern, thickness, and color.

In addition to wood and synthetic finishes, stainless-steel and powder-coated, anodized, or enameled metals are increasingly being used for cabinetry in contemporary designs.

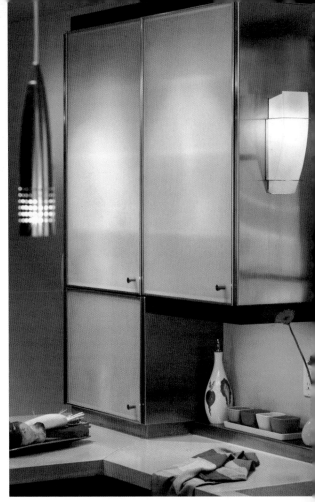

UNIFYING DETAILS (ABOVE) For an unfitted look, this kitchen's custom oak cabinets boast a light antique-chamois color with a hand-rubbed finish, while the peninsula and built-in hutch are stained dark to match the home's woodwork.

METAL WORKS (ABOVE) Though most cabinets feature a wood finish, metal finishes are at home in a contemporary kitchen. Opaque door panels with thin metal trim highlight the modern design.

AGE GRACEFULLY (LEFT) New cabinets that sport an aged finish look at home in period-style homes. Factory-applied finishes mimic a timeworn look, or for an even more authentic replication finish pieces by hand.

STATELY GEORGIAN (ABOVE) To achieve a traditional Georgian style, the cabinetry in this kitchen boasts authentic, handcarved detailing on everything from the island to the corbels.

trim & details

STYLISH SUPPORT (ABOVE) Though these corbels are decorative, their size and visual weight make them look as if they are supporting the countertop above. Such architectural pieces lend character to cabinets.

TO TOP IT OFF. The little things complete the look of your kitchen cabinetry. Take the top of the cabinets, for instance. If a cabinet tops out below the ceiling or soffit, it is often left unadorned. Run a narrow cornice along the top, however, and you have an element that's interesting and eyecatching. Enhance the look of cabinets that run to the ceiling with the addition of crown moldings or stamped trim.

Toe-kicks are candidates for stylish alterations too. Rectangular toe-kicks are standard with most cabinets, but small modifications create unique additions to the design.

Carved hardwood details such as onlays, corbels, fluted columns, reeded half-rounds, spindle caps, and furniturelike feet transform standard cabinets into one-of-a-kind design statements. Such architectural elements are especially effective on islands, but you can use them to dress up hoods and mantels over the cooking center too.

IN THE DETAILS (ABOVE) Cabinetry manufacturers are offering more add-ons, such as this turned leg, that give standard selections the appearance of handcrafted cabinetry.

DESIGN UNITY (LEFT) Corbels, turned legs, and other flourishes would be out of place on these clean-lined cabinets, which boast trim and other details that match the style of the rest of the kitchen.

SLEEK AND CLEAN (LEFT) These long stainless-steel drawer pulls create an accentuated horizontal line that is a characteristic mark of contemporary design.

MECHANICALLY MODERN (LEFT) Brushed nickel drawer pulls extend the machine-made quality of the gray door fronts. The pulls are mounted on the top edge of the drawers for increased visual interest.

COLORFUL ACCENTS (LEFT) Lend character to your cabinetry with handpainted knobs, such as these from South Africa. They beautifully complement the French blue cabinet finish.

SIMPLE DETAILS (RIGHT) The understated elegance of these matte-black finish drawer pulls and cabinet knobs allow the white cabinets and leaded-glass door inserts to take center stage.

WHIMSICAL SHAPE
(RIGHT) Though subtle, the shape of these pulls lends a lighthearted design element. Choose such hardware with care, however, as unusual shapes can be difficult to grasp.

MIX AND MATCH (ABOVE) Two styles of pulls—a crystal knob on the top drawer and bin-style pulls on the lower two—add visual variety to an island.

hardware

MAKE THEM COUNT. More than a mere mechanical necessity, cabinet hardware contributes to the overall impact of your kitchen design. While no particular rules guide hardware selection, keep sight of the overall impression you want your cabinetry to make. For instance, with Shaker-style cabinetry, try a single brass knob on each door and drawer. To capture contemporary style sleek horizontal pulls or handles in brushed chrome or stainless steel might fit better. Of course how practical the hardware is matters too. Regardless how flashy the hardware is, if it makes opening your cabinets a pain, it's not worth the trouble.

IT HINGES ON THIS. Hinge choice is affected by how your doors fit the cabinet. Inset doors are best mounted with hinges on the outside surface or with butt or wraparound hinges. Rabbeted doors are usually installed with lipped hinges. Overlay doors should be hung with invisible Eurostyle hinges. Remember that any part of the hinge that shows should complement the rest of the hardware.

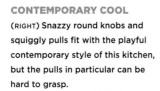

CONTEMPORARY COOL

(RIGHT) Snazzy round knobs and
squiggly pulls fit with the playful
contemporary style of this kitchen,
but the pulls in particular can be
hard to grasp.

hinges on
design

**How your door is attached to the
cabinet case dictates which
hinge styles to use.**

▸ **SURFACE HINGES** fit inset doors
and go well with country and period
decors. Keep in mind that they aren't
adjustable and require a latch
to keep the door closed.

▸ **BUTT HINGES** are often used with
period-style doors and require a
latch or catch as well.

▸ **WRAPAROUND HINGES** have a flange
inside the door that provides support
for heavy inset doors.

▸ **LIPPED HINGES** fit rabbeted doors
and any design with which an
exposed hinge pin is appropriate.

▸ **EUROSTYLE HINGES** are the standard
for overlay doors.

GOOD COMPANIONS These drawer's frosted-glass insert, small spindle pulls, and dark stain create a modern look.

ATTRACTIVE OPPOSITES (LEFT & ABOVE) Nothing says pulls and handles have to match. These oblong pulls (*left*) and round knobs (*above*) are installed on the top doors and bottom drawers, respectively, of the same cabinets. They are consistently rustic in their appearance, but the different shapes lend interest to the installation.

surfaces

Surface treatments—the materials on floors, countertops, walls, and ceilings—are the skin of the kitchen. Such elements must endure daily use with grace and charm, all the while supporting the specific style of your kitchen. With material options limited only by your budget, the opportunities for finding the perfect treatment for every surface are almost endless.

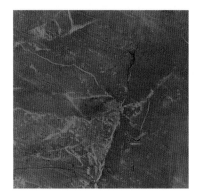
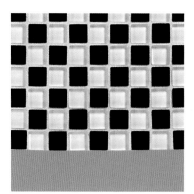

floors

HARD WORKERS. Kitchen floors take all kinds of abuse. They're the most heavily used surface in the room, so they must be durable; yet they also have to feel comfortable underfoot and enhance the style of your kitchen. When you shop for flooring, remember to consider upkeep and durability before you select a material that you love.

CHOICES. *Ceramic* and *stone tiles* are available in a range of shapes and sizes and offer durability and texture. In addition, ceramic and stone tiles are available for countertops and blacksplashes so you can match those elements to your flooring.

For the look of wood or stone patterns, consider *laminate* flooring. Essentially a plywood core with a tough synthetic top layer, laminates are virtually stainproof and never need waxing. However, laminate flooring can scratch and dent.

Vinyl offers an inexpensive alternative to other flooring with lots of attractive patterns. Modern vinyls wear well and clean up easily too.

Not to be confused with vinyl, *linoleum* is made of natural components and is far more durable than vinyl, although linoleum tiles have seam lines that may trap dirt and moisture.

Most of today's *hardwood* floors, both solid wood and engineered, come with finishes suitable for use in the kitchen. And nothing beats wood for creating rich warm overtones to a design.

Other flooring options that are gaining a foothold in the kitchen are *concrete*, which mimics natural stone and can be dyed almost any color, and *cork tiles*, which are cushiony, noiseless, and durable.

COOL CORK (ABOVE) Two colors of cork tiles form a checkerboard design on this floor. Cork, a renewable material, can last for decades. Regular maintenance only requires sweeping and mopping, although the urethane finish must be sanded off and reapplied every few years.

WOOD AND STONE (BELOW) Use different flooring to define open rooms. Here large-scale 24-inch-square limestone tiles define the breakfast area, while the kitchen floor is quartersawn maple. Stone tiles require periodic sealing; hardwood may need refinishing.

WORKING WONDERS Ceramic tile comes in so many sizes and shapes that it works magic in any kitchen. Large porcelain tiles, here in a neutral tone, serve well as a backdrop that shows off the rest of the kitchen. Ceramic tile is incredibly hard and can be cold—consider installing electric heat mats on the subflooring before the tile is set.

INTERESTING ENGINEERING

(LEFT) An engineered hardwood floor features a layer of real hardwood over layers of plywood or high-density fiberboard. This floor doesn't expand and contract with heat and humidity like solid hardwood floors do.

LOWERING THE GRADE

(BELOW) Flooring lumber is graded on appearance rather than strength. A lower grade will have more knots and blemishes but is still as strong as higher grades—and it might be just what a country or rustic kitchen requires.

IS IT REAL? (ABOVE) Modern laminates are engineered not only for durability and low cost but also to look so good that it's hard to distinguish whether the flooring is laminate or real wood.

DISTINCTIVE STATEMENT (BELOW) The same flooring material is used in these adjacent rooms, but the spaces are distinguished from one another by different tile patterns and colors.

COLORFUL DEFINITION (RIGHT) Intricate ceramic tile patterns adorn this kitchen floor. From a distance, the pattern under the dining table looks like an area rug. The tile color is similar to that of the nearby wood floor for an easy transition between the two.

SMART GROOVES
This handsome cherry countertop has drain grooves to the sink so water doesn't pool on the countertop. Use mineral oil to protect the finish.

countertops & backsplashes

DOUBLE DUTY. Countertops must withstand almost as much action as floors. And, not surprisingly, they're also a major kitchen design element. Backsplashes don't get much of a workout, but they are an important style element and are useful for protecting your walls from stains, nicks, and other minor mishaps. Use the same material for your countertops and backsplashes for a unified look, or make a statement by using different materials on each.

DESIGN POTENTIAL. *Laminate* is one of the least expensive countertop options and comes in a variety of colors, textures, and patterns. This easy-to-clean surface is vulnerable to stains, sharp knives, and hot pans.

Ceramic tile is durable and dramatic, and the variety of shapes and colors available makes it ideal for creating patterns. The tile itself is easy to clean, but the grouted joints between tiles collect dirt and are prone to staining.

Despite their high price tag, *natural stones* such as granite, marble, and soapstone are popular for their elegance, versatility, and durability.

Solid-surfacing is a sheet of synthetic material resembling stone that can be molded to fit any kitchen layout and style. It is lighter and easier to work with than natural stone, although knives and hot pans can scratch and burn it.

Other materials steadily making inroads into the countertop and backsplash domain include stainless steel, hardwoods, synthetic quartz, concrete, and butcher block.

COPPER AND CLAY
(RIGHT) Hammered copper and clay tiles create a rustic pattern for this kitchen backsplash.

INSET INTEREST
(RIGHT) This row of inset mosaic glass tiles break up an expanse of larger matte-finish tiles.

GLEAMING GLASS (BELOW) Rustic Italian glass mosaic tiles create a striking backsplash behind a cooktop. Backsplash materials can be less durable than countertop materials.

SPECIALTY FEATURES Glass blocks allow light to spill onto a stainless-steel countertop and serve as an easy-care backsplash. Stainless steel looks great when paired with commercial appliances and cleans well, but it does scratch easily.

FAUX STONE (ABOVE) Engineered stone countertops mimic natural materials but encompass a much larger color selection than natural stone. Quartz, the primary ingredient in engineered stone countertops, has the strength and durability of granite.

UNIFYING DETAILS (ABOVE) Butcher block makes a great countertop and cutting surface. Slots routed into this island countertop allow crumbs to drop into the removable drawer below.

the tall and **short of it**

It used to be that countertops were always positioned 36 inches off the floor, but today's designs don't hold countertop height sacrosanct—with good reason.

A 36-inch countertop makes a comfortable work surface for most tasks if the cook is of average height. Even so it makes sense to have at least two counter heights in your kitchen for different uses and functions, with one 28 to 36 inches off the floor and the other 36 to 45 inches above the floor. If the main cook is taller or shorter by a significant amount, changing the countertop height makes working more comfortable. Taller cooks, for example, feel more comfortable working at a surface that's 38 inches or higher. In addition to individual variations, certain kitchen activities are better suited to specific heights. For baking prep, rolling dough is easier on a surface 29 to 31 inches high. Dishwashing may be more comfortable with a countertop 38 to 40 inches above the floor, especially if the sink is deep. All of these individual heights can be built into your design from the start. Just remember that such alterations will affect the dimensions of the cabinets below. For instance a standard dishwasher probably won't fit under a lowered snack center.

NOVEL HARLEQUIN (ABOVE) No material offers as many design possibilities as ceramic tile. This harlequin backsplash has been carefully set so the colors are randomly distributed. The blue tiles contrast with the red and cream tones, both of which are also found in the laminate countertop.

WHITE TILE DONE RIGHT (RIGHT) Stylish backsplashes lend personality to the kitchen. This crackle-glaze tile backsplash features an ornate relief design inspired by antique ironwork.

GO FOR GRANITE (RIGHT)
The cost of granite countertops varies greatly depending on quality, thickness, and availability of the variety you choose. Edge treatments such as this popular bullnose look may increase the cost.

TILE TONES (BELOW) Textured ceramic tile is particularly useful for kitchen countertops because it withstands hot pots and pans without scorching and resists moisture from splashes or puddles around the sink. The grout lines, however, are prone to staining.

all for one?

Before you decide on a single material for all of your kitchen countertops, consider where different materials may be more effective than others.

▸ **BUTCHER BLOCK** works well in the food preparation area—particularly on an island—for chopping chores and bread slicing.

▸ **MARBLE** is best for rolling dough, but if you don't want to spend the money on a permanent slab, purchase a small section to create a mobile baking center.

▸ **CERAMIC TILE** or granite located near the cooking center is a durable, heat-resistant spot for hot pans.

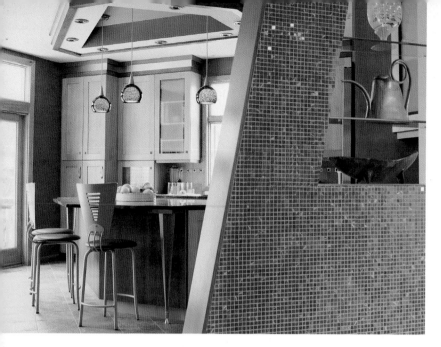

PERFECT ENTRANCE (LEFT) An angled wall clad in tile leads the way into this contemporary kitchen. The coffered ceiling over the island continues the sharp-edge geometry.

walls & ceilings

THINK OPTIONS. In many kitchens, walls and ceilings function simply as a backdrop for cabinetry and appliances. However, as with every element in the kitchen, their appearance contributes to the overall look of the space.

Painting or wallpapering are easy ways to give walls a splash of color, but other options also dress up walls and ceilings with texture and dimension.

POSSIBILITIES. If you choose *paint*, select a semigloss paint for walls and a glossy paint for trim—both wipe clean with ease.

Ceramic tile made for walls is thinner and less expensive than floor tile. Floor tiles also work on walls, as long as the wall can withstand the extra weight.

From beaded board to polished walnut panels, *wood* spells quality and durability. Be sure to apply an appropriate finish because wood is subject to water damage.

Other creative options include hanging *solid-surface* panels for stylish low-maintenance walls. *Glass block* creates interesting architectural patterns and ushers in light. Or try *brick*, which is available in a variety of colors, textures, and thicknesses perfect for creating unique patterns.

OVERHEAD INTEREST (BELOW) Wood beams create architectural interest and infuse rustic style.

DRAMATIC ACCENT
This glazed-tile mural with its
array of peaches creates
a dramatic point of interest
on a dark painted wall.

COOK'S CASTLE The combination of large cleft-limestone columns and walls with a brick backsplash is a study in textural contrasts that never loses its visual interest.

JUST PICTURE IT (ABOVE) A painted wall
provides a neutral background for a collection
of paintings and sculpted objects. Displaying
artwork and collections is great ways to dress
up wall surfaces.

WOOD TONES
(LEFT) Dark beams
make a kitchen with
a high ceiling appear
more intimate. The
entire design is unified
with wood cabinets,
plank flooring, and a
refinished utility table.

sinks &
faucets

Nothing in a kitchen works harder than your sink and faucet. They're the two fixtures expected to perform without fail in almost every aspect of kitchen life from food prep to cleaning—in fact, they're such an integral part of the kitchen that some spaces include two. Choose your sink and faucet with care because style counts just as much as quality.

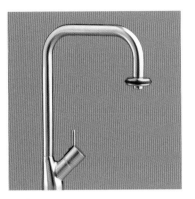

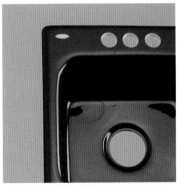

BLACK MAGIC (ABOVE) The black double-bowl, enameled undermount sink virtually disappears into its wood and granite countertop surroundings.

BETTER BASINS (BELOW) Stainless-steel sinks are a practical kitchen choice. This smaller basin, where the garbage disposal is located, is useful for food prep, while the larger basin is ideal for filling and washing pots.

sink materials

EXPRESSIONS. Not long ago, what sink material you used in your kitchen was an easy decision. You could select porcelain, cast iron, or stainless steel. With more emphasis on individual expression, however, today's kitchen needs a sink that's not only a workhorse but also an indication of personality. And as modern improvements have met that demand, the result is an explosion of quality materials.

MATERIALS. *Stainless steel* still tops the popularity charts. Be sure your stainless-steel model has thick walls and contains a high percentage of nickel and chromium.

For shine, color, and durability, select *porcelain-enamel cast iron*. It's extremely heavy and holds water temperature far longer than most materials.

Solid-surface sinks are easy to care for, resist scratches and chips, and are available in virtually any color.

Quartz- or *granite-resin composites* feature a beautiful speckled color and are resistant to damage as long as you don't use abrasive cleaners.

Often found in country-kitchen settings, *fireclay* is a dense, durable, low-maintenance choice.

Vitreous china is hard and nonporous with a glasslike shine, but it's difficult to mold large items such as double-bowl kitchen sinks from this material.

Metal sinks—particularly copper and brass—impart a warm look that is just right for both traditional and contemporary designs.

Easy-to-clean, durable *stone*, such as soapstone, slate, and granite, is another popular sink choice.

DOUBLE DUTY (ABOVE) Undermount sinks allow a modern stainless-steel basin to be incorporated into traditional decor. For design continuity, select similar sink and faucet styles for both the primary and secondary sinks.

UNIVERSAL COMPLEMENT (ABOVE)
Black is a color suited to any decor, as this enameled cast-iron sink demonstrates. Its tough surface keeps its shine for years and cleans up quickly.

VINTAGE CURVE
(LEFT) Hammered copper and a curved-neck faucet lend a vintage look to this island prep sink.

INTEGRAL APPEARANCE (LEFT)
Solid-surfacing is known for its stonelike beauty and nonporous surface. This sink, integrated with a solid-surface countertop, creates a seamless, easy-to-clean setup.

ALL FIRED UP (BELOW) Fireclay sinks are made from a clay base fired at intense heat to produce a durable, glossy finish. The material resists scratches and abrasions, although it can stain over time. This apron-front version was handmade in France.

LOVELY IN LIMESTONE This limestone apron-front sink offers only one bowl, but the ample size of most farmhouse sinks makes them ideal for cleaning large items.

sink shapes

BOWL GAMES. Manufacturers have responded to changing kitchen practices with an array of bowl configurations.

Single-basin sinks are useful for small kitchens or as a second sink in a large kitchen with a dedicated food prep area. Recent models are wider and deeper to handle large pots and other kitchen tools with ease. Shapes include rectangles, ovals, circles, and more, so you can choose a sink that's visually interesting and convenient.

Double-basin units are available in standard models, but new configurations with customized bowl shapes and sizes are also popular.

Triple-basin sinks typically offer two large basins—perfect for stacking dishes—with one small, shallow bowl between them.

Choose your sink based on how you use it. Deeper bowls with straight sides and a flat bottom provide more usable space and make it easier to stack dishes. Offset drains free up storage directly under the sink. To wash large baking pans, choose a bowl big enough to soak them.

COOL CURVES (ABOVE) The curve between the two bowls of this antique nickel sink is practical and pretty. It provides a spot for the cylindrical drain stoppers that raise to fill the bowls and lower to empty them.

PRACTICAL TRADITION (BELOW) A large two-bowl sink provides plenty of versatility. Different sizes of bowls cater to different tasks.

SINK RIGHT IN (RIGHT) Straight sides and a flat bottom increase the working space in a sink dramatically. Install a tall faucet spout, and a deep sink is ready for almost any kitchen task.

sink installation

CLEANUP AND STYLE. The mounting of your kitchen sink depends on the form of the sink itself.

Self-rimming sinks are supported by a rim that rests on the edges of a hole cut in the countertop. Although the joint where the rim and countertop meet is sealed with caulk, cleanup here requires more attention than other styles. The edges of the raised sink act as a barrier when you try to sweep crumbs into the basin.

Undermount sinks are anchored to the underside of the counter to create a sleek, unbroken line from counter to basin. Because no sink rim interferes, cleanup is easier. This style of sink is a popular companion for solid-surfacing and stone countertops because it requires a waterproof countertop material.

Integral sinks are formed from the same material as the countertop to create one unit with no visible joints between the two. In the past, integral sinks were constructed only in solid-surface countertops. Now stainless steel and natural stone provide integral options.

Flush-mounted sinks have edges that are level with the countertop. This method is an option with ceramic tile countertops.

Farmhouse sinks come with a finished apron that is left exposed. Some are made for undermount installations; others are self-rimming. Many farmhouse sinks come without a deck, so the faucet must be mounted on the countertop behind or beside the sink bowl.

JUST DROP IN (ABOVE) A self-rimming sink is the easiest to install. A layer of caulk is applied under the edge of the rim and the sink is dropped into the hole. Self-rimming sinks are a bit more difficult to keep clean around the edges than other styles.

HIGH STYLE (BELOW) A black granite countertop provides a stylish frame for this polished stainless-steel undermount sink. Stones such as granite make good surfaces for undermount sinks because the exposed edges are waterproof.

PERFECT PATINA
This undermount farmhouse sink required expert fitting of the countertop because the edges are exposed.

MADE FOR EACH OTHER This pot-filler faucet and deep sink basin work in tandem to make filling pots easy. The smaller basin to the right keeps produce that has been rinsed out of the way.

faucets

FUNCTIONAL STYLES. Faucets are more stylish and dependable than ever, with everything from long, tall spouts for filling pots to pullout faucets that make kitchen tasks easier. Whatever their style, faucets come with one of four basic types of valves: ceramic disk, cartridge, ball, and compression.

Single-handle disk faucets are typically the most durable and trouble-free. *Cartridge* faucets come in single- or double-handle configurations and are easy to fix or replace when leaks occur. In *single-handle ball* faucets, a rotating ball inside permits water to flow, regulates the flow of hot and cold water, and shuts off the water altogether. *Compression* faucets control water flow by compressing a rubber washer against an orifice in the valve stem.

FABULOUS FINISHES. Faucets are often available in polished or brushed finishes—polished finishes tend to stand out more, while brushed finishes are more subdued. *Chrome* ranks as one of the most popular faucet finishes because it holds up well and doesn't require protective coatings to keep it gleaming. With a machined brass body, an electroplated chrome faucet lasts a lifetime. *Brass* faucets feature coatings that make them nearly indestructible. In addition *nickel*, *pewter*, *gold*, and other metals offer both polished and brushed surfaces. Another option is *epoxy*, which is available in a host of colors that are spectacularly modern and work well with contemporary designs.

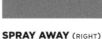

SPRAY AWAY (RIGHT) Faucets with pullout spray heads make rinsing foods and cleaning up easier.

STYLISH AND EASY (RIGHT) One handle is easier than two (and safer for the kids). This model boasts a contemporary touch.

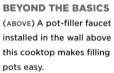
BEYOND THE BASICS
(ABOVE) A pot-filler faucet installed in the wall above this cooktop makes filling pots easy.

HISTORY MOUNTED (ABOVE) A wall-mount faucet looks era-appropriate when paired with an apron-front sink. It also frees up space for washing large pots and pans.

AUTHENTIC AIR (LEFT) An antique faucet and a sprayer with an authentic patina look at home paired with a teak countertop and an aged-copper undermount sink.

DOUBLE DUTY (BELOW) This unit combines a restaurant-style faucet with a flexible sprayer as well as a more traditional faucet. Both facilitate tasks above an extra-deep cleanup sink.

faucet
innovations

Today's faucets include a host of new features to make kitchen tasks easier.

High-arc faucets and pullout spouts contribute a heap of convenience to kitchen chores. But faucet innovation doesn't stop there.

Some pullout spouts come with a pause button to interrupt the flow of water as you move from one container to another without wetting everything in between.

A number of built-in water filtration devices dispense filtered water for cooking and drinking.

If you don't want to wait for the hot water to reach the faucet from the water heater, or if you frequently enjoy drinking hot beverages, consider installing an instant hot-water dispenser. Chilled-water dispensers are also available, as are combination units that deliver both hot and cold water instantly.

FUNCTIONAL COMBO (ABOVE) A pullout spray head is a functional update for an otherwise traditional faucet, particularly when paired with a built-in soap dispenser.

appliances

Every kitchen requires some combination of tools—such as ranges, refrigerators, microwaves, and dishwashers—to function properly. Choosing the right appliances for your kitchen requires consideration of dimensions, functions, and features. With a little bit of know-how, finding the right appliances won't be a chore—it will be an adventure.

ranges

WHAT'S IN A NAME? Ranges are often called stoves and vice versa. The words are synonymous—they mean a cooking unit with an oven on the bottom and some form of cooking surface on top. Beyond the basic functions of a range, however, the options available are many.

FUELS AND FANCIES. The type of fuel source a range uses is a primary distinction—gas, electricity, or a combination of the two with a dual-fuel model that pairs a gas cooktop with an electric oven. Each comes with its own advantages and disadvantages. Gas traditionally has been the most economical choice and can be turned on instantly. Electric ranges have coil elements that accommodate almost any cookware and are often easier to clean.

Both types of ranges are available as freestanding units, slide-in units that don't have side panels, or drop-in units that sit on a platform with edges sealed for easier cleaning.

Ranges tend to last 10 to 15 years and endure a lot of wear and tear during that time. Look for porcelain broiler pans, heavy-duty oven racks that support roasts and large casseroles, and durable dishwasher-safe grids.

off the rack or **go pro?**

Get the look of a commercial-style range for less.

Commercial ranges make a strong visual impression in any kitchen and are particularly attractive for serious cooks. True commercial ranges like those in restaurants are costly; require equally pricey accessories, including a high-capacity vent; and need extra insulation for the side and rear clearances because the ranges are uninsulated.

If you're not that serious about having a commercial range, consider purchasing a professional-style version that combines the power, the precision, and some of the features of commercial appliances in a package designed for home use.

Or if you want the appearance of a professional-grade range without the high price tag, consider one of the top-end residential ranges covered in stainless steel and beefed up with professional-looking upgrades. They have professional style for considerably less cost.

FREESTANDING FUNCTIONS
(BELOW) This freestanding electric range features a large oven interior perfect for cooking large dishes or even entire meals.

ALL WHITE (ABOVE)
Professional-style ranges are not limited to stainless steel, as this white range demonstrates. A professional-style range typically features high-capacity and simmer burners, a grill or griddle, continuous grates, and a convection oven.

WARM UP (RIGHT) Some ranges come equipped with a warming oven, which is particularly convenient when preparing large meals.

ROOM FOR TWO

(RIGHT) Double wall
ovens create efficient
workspaces that may be
located just outside the
main cooking area.

PLEASING PARTNER

(BELOW) Built into the
cabinetry within the work
triangle, a convection
oven and microwave oven
make a functional pair.
Locate the oven near a
stretch of countertop
so you have a place to
set hot dishes you pull
from it.

BEST OF BOTH WORLDS
(RIGHT) Rather than purchasing a range with a stove and oven in one unit, more homeowners are combining a gas cooktop with a separate undercounter convection oven.

ovens

IMPROVED DESIGN. Today's ovens come in a variety of configurations and sizes and with an increasing number of amenities.

Standard electric or gas ovens are also called radiant-heat or thermal ovens. They typically have one heating source on the bottom for baking and roasting and another on top for broiling.

Convection ovens differ from standard ovens in that they use fans to circulate heated air. Convection reduces cooking time, results in better browning and baking, and produces juicier meats and crustier breads. Convection ovens, however, must be monitored more closely than standard models to avoid overcooking. Many homeowners choose a wall oven that offers both conventional and convection cooking.

Wall ovens save on counterspace because they fit in base cabinets or in narrow units designed specifically for this purpose. Because your oven will likely see less use than other appliances, you can locate it outside the main cooking area—an excellent opportunity to create a separate baking center.

If you prepare large meals, entertain often, or have two cooks frequently using the kitchen at the same time, you may wish to include two ovens. An undercounter model is a good choice for a second oven when two cooks are at work.

BLACK BEAUTY
(RIGHT) This pair of built-in ovens looks particularly striking in black. Regardless of appliance color, choose an oven with a large, clear window and a strong interior light so you can check on cooking food without frequently opening the oven door.

cooktops

COUNTERTOP COOKING. For more flexibility in function and design than you can get with a range, pair a cooktop with one or more wall ovens. The cooking surface is one of the focal points of the kitchen work triangle, so plan placement carefully. If your kitchen includes a centrally located island, you may choose to place your cooktop there.

Regardless of where the cooktop is located, plan for ample counterspace around the cooktop. At a minimum you want 12 inches of counterspace on one side of the cooking area and at least 15 inches on the other. For safety reasons the countertop should also extend a minimum of 9 inches behind the cooking surface. Also plan for counterspace in front of the cooktop.

FUEL CHOICES. Decide whether you want a gas or electric cooktop. Standard models for either type can be dropped into the countertop and are hooked up from below. Most are outfitted with four burners—although you may find models with as many as eight burners. Models are available that allow you to interchange the burners for grills, griddles, or accessories.

The options for electric cooktops are particularly impressive. On some, smooth ceramic glass covers traditional heating coils. In a solid-element cooktop cast-iron disks cover the coils. Halogen burners rely on high heat developed by halogen light. With induction cooking induction coils below the surface cause an electromagnetic field to heat up.

VERSATILE COOKING (ABOVE) Five gas burners in this cooktop provide plenty of easily controlled heat for a cook who likes to entertain or prepare complex dishes.

WHERE IT'S AT
(LEFT) A cooktop set in the counter allows room for storage of pots, pans, and cooking utensils directly below. Be sure to plan for proper ventilation above the cooking area.

TUCKED AWAY
(LEFT) This island includes two integral sinks, a cooktop, a built-in steamer, and drawers for cookware in a compact cooking area. A tall cabinet at the end of the island visually blocks the cooktop from the living room.

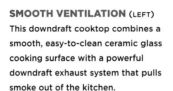

SMOOTH VENTILATION (LEFT)
This downdraft cooktop combines a smooth, easy-to-clean ceramic glass cooking surface with a powerful downdraft exhaust system that pulls smoke out of the kitchen.

vents

EFFICIENCY AND DESIGN. Once considered a luxury, a ventilation system is now a necessity in modern kitchens for removing moisture, steam, and grease-laden air. In addition to keeping your kitchen cleaner, healthier, and cooler, ventilation hoods also present another kitchen design opportunity.

UP OR DOWN. Ventilation systems rely on updraft or downdraft technology.

Updraft units are located above the cooktop and feature a hood that collects the air and moves it though a duct, either to a filter or outside the house. Venting to the outside is the better of the two options, although it is more expensive. In a filtered system the air passes through a filter designed to remove grease and then the uncooled air is recirculated back into the kitchen. These filters require periodic cleaning but most can be placed in the dishwasher.

Downdraft systems do what their name implies—they take air down from the cooking surface and move it down through a filter or to the outside. Some downdraft systems are built as an integral part of the cooktop. Others rely on vents installed almost flush with the countertop—push a button and the vents raise up to draw in the air. How large a ventilation system you need depends on the size of your cooking area and the meals you prepare.

SPECTACULAR CYLINDER
(ABOVE) A custom cylindrical hood provides a sculptural focal point for this compact kitchen.

UNOBSTRUCTED VIEWS (ABOVE) A stainless-steel hood over the cooktop anchors this kitchen island. Its sleek, narrow configuration allows clear views of the gardens outside the kitchen windows.

BEAUTIFUL THINKING (LEFT)
In keeping with the subdued color palette, this custom range hood is the same putty color as the cabinets.

refrigerators & freezers

SIZE WISE. Consider your refrigerator selection carefully—refrigerators can operate for 15 years or more, so remember to plan for changes in family size. Measure the height, width, and depth of your available refrigerator space. Also consider the capacity of the appliance. A family of two generally requires 8 to 10 cubic feet of fresh food space and 4 cubic feet of freezer space; for each additional family member, increase food capacity an extra cubic foot in the refrigerator and an extra 2 cubic feet in the freezer.

When in the store, be sure to check the noise level of the refrigerator as well as each model's Energy Star label to determine the average energy use per year.

KEY CONFIGURATIONS. Top-mount freezer units are the most efficient and least costly models, but they aren't as accessible as units with the freezer on the bottom. Consider a bottom freezer section that has a pull-open drawer for easy use. Side-by-side models also provide great access but might not hold bulkier items as easily as you want.

Freestanding units are a little larger than most cabinet depths, so they stick out a few inches from a standard 24-inch cabinet run. Shallow models that extend about as far as standard cabinet fronts look better than refrigerators that bump out beyond countertops. Built-in units are made 24 inches deep to eliminate this problem.

In small kitchens or for extra convenience, consider built-in refrigerator or freezer drawers that fit 24-inch base cabinets.

MATCHING CABINETRY (ABOVE)
Wooden trim panels are sometimes used to disguise refrigerators so they are virtually indistinguishable from the surrounding cabinets.

accessories

Your options for refrigerator features are many. Here are a few worth considering.

▶ **STORAGE ELEMENTS** include adjustable-height and pullout glass shelves, see-through drawers, large adjustable door bins, and sliding freezer baskets. Spillproof shelves reduce cleanup.

▶ **BEVERAGE HELPERS** such as built-in ice and water dispensers—some with filters—make access to cold drinks easy.

▶ **HIGH-TECH OPTIONS** including digital displays show internal temperatures at a glance and make changing them as easy as pushing a button. Separate controls allow you to set different areas of the refrigerator or freezer at specific temperatures.

EASY ACCESS (BELOW) A French door refrigerator with a bottom freezer keeps fresh food as well as a water and ice dispenser at eye level and frozen food in a glide-out drawer below.

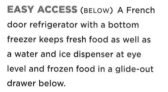

SHALLOW FIT (ABOVE) Cabinet-depth refrigerators are ideal for kitchens with limited floor space. Here a shallow refrigerator allows ample room between an island and the appliance.

IT'S IN THE DRAWER Stacked dishwasher drawers make cleanup easy. Heavy-duty items can be loaded in one drawer and more delicate items in another. Cabinetry-matching panels ensure that dishwasher drawers look like traditional storage.

dishwashers

EASY CLEAN. Taking care of dirty dishes is never fun, but it's a whole lot easier with the right dishwasher. Choose from built-in, portable, full-size, and compact models.

Generally install the dishwasher beneath the counter either to the right or left of the main sink. For large families or frequent entertaining, install a second dishwasher nearby. Or consider dishwasher drawers, which fit conveniently under countertops. To save water, wash smaller loads of dishes or reserve one drawer for pots and pans and the other for dishware.

Today's dishwashers come with more than a few extra features, including soft-touch electronic controls, multiple wash cycles and types, adjustable-height racks, and matching panels so the dishwasher blends with your cabinetry.

Before buying check the sprayer mechanism design (high-performance dishwashers have two or three spray arms) and the drain system (a twin-pump system drains dirty water faster than a standard single pump). Beyond these features, also take note of noise levels and how much energy your dishwasher will expend.

NO STOOPING (ABOVE)
A raised dishwasher paired with a lowered double sink makes cleanup duties easier because less stooping is required.

microwaves

FOR THOSE ON THE GO. Microwave ovens offer cooking speed and convenience in a compact unit. They're the appliance of choice for warming up leftovers, cooking quick snacks, and defrosting foods for dinner. Some kitchens even sport two—one in the main cooking area and another in a designated snack zone.

Microwave ovens are made as freestanding units or as built-ins for cabinets over the range or near the cooking center. Built-in units exhaust moisture and hot air out the front of the unit. Freestanding microwaves exhaust the air to the rear and should never be mounted in an enclosed cabinet unless it allows for unrestricted airflow.

Units are available in a multitude of power ranges. Although you can save money by purchasing a lower-power unit, you're better off buying at least a 1,000-watt model with 1.5 cubic feet of cooking space inside. A turntable is helpful for cooking evenly. Some units also include a convection option, multiple power levels, and a steam sensor that stops the cooking process when it senses the food is done.

SNACK CENTRAL

(ABOVE) An additional microwave allows family members to make snacks without getting in the way of the main cooking activities.

KEEPING IT HANDY (LEFT)

Conveniently located in the main cooking area, a microwave makes short work of warming leftovers and defrosting foods. Many come equipped with controls that set the proper timing for selected foods.

COMPACT UNIT

(ABOVE) Apothecary drawers store spices and cooking tools around the microwave. A cabinet that encloses a freestanding microwave must be open in the back to allow for air flow.

lighting

Think bright illumination or a gentle glow. Nothing sheds light on a kitchen like a well-placed lamp or wall sconce. Lighting is key for seeing what's cooking and for setting the mood. Fixtures are beacons of style—a sleek pendant provides a contemporary touch, while a decorative chandelier makes a traditional kitchen shine.

LIGHT SOURCES (ABOVE)
Recessed downlights, decorative ceiling fixtures, and natural light sources all contribute to a pleasing kitchen environment. To avoid glare, recessed lights should have a reflector or baffle. Decorative fixtures with dimmers match light intensity to the task and the mood.

kitchen light needs

FILL THE ROOM. Kitchens are often described as bright and cheery, and for good reason. Typically the center of the American home, kitchens provide a space for socializing and evoke fond memories of dinners with family and friends. Good lighting contributes to these positive associations. Preparing meals, dining, and cleaning up are all activities that require ample light.

A kitchen filled with multiple light sources provides the flexibility necessary to adjust lighting for the task. Fluorescent or low-voltage incandescent lights mounted under cabinets illuminate countertop work surfaces when food is being prepared. For intimate dinners, turn off the undercabinet lights, dim recessed ambient lights, and bathe the dining table in the soft glow of a chandelier.

LIGHTING DESIGN. The size of your kitchen, colors of cabinets and walls, ceiling height, and natural light sources all impact the choice and placement of light fixtures. Dark cabinet finishes, for example, will absorb light, requiring closer spacing of downlights than a kitchen with white cabinets. Rooms with a maximum of 9-foot ceilings require smaller diameter recessed lights than a space with a vaulted ceiling.

INVITING SPACE Multiple light sources illuminate this kitchen with a welcoming glow. Each work surface is washed in light. Recessed downlights provide ambient illumination throughout the room.

TIGHT SQUEEZE (LEFT)
Sconces mounted directly to the window frame rather than the wall allow the window to fill maximum wall space while still providing an evening light source.

planning for light

LIGHT AND DESIGN. Step into any attractive kitchen, day or night, and you'll find that one of the elements that contributes to its allure is the way it is lit. It may rely on light streaming through the windows, electric lighting, or a combination of both, but behind every well-designed kitchen is a lighting plan that both enhances its appearance and puts light where you need it for specific tasks.

MULTIPLE SOURCES. One long-standing method of lighting a kitchen relies on a strong, bright light source in the middle of the ceiling that casts light throughout the room. While such central lighting illuminates a good deal of the kitchen area, when you're between it and a work surface, you're working in your own shadow. Specific light sources solve this problem. Track lights over a sink or prep center do the trick, as do pendants, spotlights, or recessed floods in the ceiling above the work area. The same holds true for any area of the kitchen. Create a lighting plan that makes kitchen work comfortable, eliminates shadows and glare, and at the same time contributes a stylistic element compatible with the rest of the room.

MULTIPLE CHOICES (ABOVE)
The lighting scheme in this urban contemporary loft fits the design and offers multiple light sources. Recessed and ceiling-mount fixtures offer ambient light while a pendant provides task light.

CLEAR CHOICE (ABOVE) Clear glass pendants offer ample light without detracting from the clean lines and streamlined design of this kitchen. Recessed lights on the perimeter of the kitchen ensure a pleasing overall brightness to the room.

SPECIALTY FIXTURES (RIGHT) This kitchen features a variety of lighting sources, including recessed lighting on the ceiling, undercabinet task lighting, and a beautiful pendent light above the kitchen table.

COMPLEMENTARY FIXTURES
(ABOVE) Fabric shades provide an artful touch to the lighting in this converted warehouse loft kitchen. A dimming system offers flexibility to adjust lights according to the amount of natural light streaming through the wall of windows.

TRANSITION TRICKS (ABOVE) Three sources of light—pendants, a table lamp, and recessed fixtures—illuminate this transition area between the kitchen and great room. The warm, neutral tones of the table and pendent lampshades create continuity between the spaces.

COUNTRY CHARM (ABOVE) A pewter-finish chandelier accents this country kitchen and illuminates the dining table. Small, low-wattage flame bulbs provide subdued lighting for intimate dinners. Ambient light throughout the kitchen casts a brighter glow for daily activities.

styles

TAKE YOUR PICK. Lights come in a variety of styles—both in terms of the type and design of the fixtures. Before you select a light because you love the shade, make sure you have the right fixture.

LAYERS OF LIGHT. *Ambient light* sources may include pendent fixtures as well as a series of recessed lights positioned around the perimeter of or throughout the room.

Task light should be designed to illuminate all work surfaces—countertops, island, sink, stove, dining area, and pantry—from above without shadows or glare.

Accent lights highlight focal points in the room such as artwork or the contents of a china cabinet.

Once you have the right mix of fixtures, have fun choosing design styles—bold, fun, subdued, classic, retro—that coordinate and enhance the overall look you want for your kitchen.

TRIPLE PLAY (ABOVE) Contemporary metal pendants above a work surface offer task lighting. Small cutouts in the shades softly filter limited ambient light.

SOFT GLOW (ABOVE) A pendent fixture with a shade in a subdued hue of the wall color offers stylish task lighting and casts a soft glow throughout the kitchen.

COPPER GLOW (LEFT) This wall-mount sconce provides task lighting for the cleanup zone and casts warm light on red cabinetry and a copper backsplash.

FADE TO THE BACKGROUND
In this space, the building's architecture takes center stage. Simple white fixtures and undercabinet lights provide sufficient light without detracting from the other strong visual elements.

choosing the **right light**

Reflectorized incandescents create a beam of soft- or hard-edged light.

Efficient, long-lasting retrofit fluorescent bulbs fit in most standard lamps.

Compact fluorescent bulbs cast a warm light and render color well.

Flame bulbs lend traditional style to chandeliers and produce low light.

In fixtures and lamps, halogen bulbs provide clear white light.

PRACTICAL CHOICE
(LEFT) A valanced drapery
is not only a stylish window
treatment; it's also a practical
choice above a sink because
it's low enough to control the
light but high enough to stay
out of the way of splashes.

windows

EYES OF THE ROOM. Make windows
a central element in your lighting plan.
The light they bring not only illuminates
the room; the sunshine also affects
the kitchen's appearance and mood. A
windowless room can be dreary. Install
windows and both the room and your
outlook become cheery. Windows also
alter the climate in a kitchen. Close them
to trap the sun's warming rays. Open
them to let fresh air in and "cooked" air
out. Well-placed windows also let you look
out on pleasing natural views.

ADMITTING LIGHT. Because windows
are the primary source for ambient light
in the kitchen, their area should be equal
to about 10 percent of the area of the
floor. In smaller kitchens with limited
exterior wall space, increase the light
with taller windows or install "eyebrow"
windows above existing ones. Skylights
(essentially windows in the roof) also
bring additional light into the kitchen.
Skylights solve lighting problems without
disturbing the design of your cabinets.

BRIGHT AND CHEERY (ABOVE) Open casement
windows bring in fresh air and ensure this breakfast
nook is a cheery place. When necessary, Roman
shades lower quickly to reduce the light without
blocking the breeze.

TRADE
OFF (ABOVE)
Maximizing the
amount of storage
space provided by
base cabinets opens
up large areas of wall
space for windows.

window **treatments**

Window treatments perform almost as many jobs in a room as the windows themselves. They increase privacy, filter light, and contribute their own stylistic character to your design.

Choose window treatments first on the basis of how much light you need to control. Sheers filter light and provide a diffused but not complete measure of privacy. Shades roll up when you don't need privacy. Fabric styles should coordinate with the rest of the room. Single-color countertops might benefit from colorful patterns on window treatments, but avoid an easily stainable fabric above a sink or preparation center.

GREAT GLOW (LEFT) This peninsula eating area benefits from the expansive windows that flood the kitchen with natural light.

KITCHEN COMFORT (RIGHT) A simple valance provides visual interest without blocking natural light from entering the kitchen.

BRIGHT DIVERSION (ABOVE) A bank of windows positioned across from the sink provides illumination as well as visual distraction from cleanup responsibilities.

ECLECTIC ILLUMINATION (ABOVE) A wash of natural light softens the contemporary style of this kitchen. Sleek track lighting above the sink provides task illumination after dark.

bringing the
outdoors in

In addition to providing views and ventilation, windows are critical components of any kitchen lighting scheme.

Factor window placement, size, and style into your kitchen lighting plans. Even if your kitchen benefits from ample windows, you still need artificial light sources after nightfall and to brighten otherwise dark nooks and corners. Fluorescent or low-voltage incandescent lights mounted under cabinets, for example, provide suitable task lighting and eliminate shadows that make it difficult to work efficiently and safely.

Window treatments impact the amount of natural light in the room. Select window treatments that maximize natural light and reduce or eliminate glare. Roman and roller shades, for instance, raise to leave most of the windowpane exposed to sunlight. Sheers filter unwelcome harsh rays.

TASK LIGHT (LEFT) A simple Roman shade maximizes the light entering through this window. Though the sink area is bright with natural light during daylight hours, recessed downlights (*not shown*) also illuminate the area.

HIGH LIGHT (ABOVE) The drama of contrasts created by the stark blacks and whites in this kitchen and dining area is thrown into high relief by the ambient light from this wide section of windows.

choosing **windows**

When making window choices, consider energy efficiency, window placement, and style.

Look for multiple-pane windows, which are the norm for energy efficiency. Some come with gasses such as argon between the panes to increase performance. Next consider how easily the window will open in its location. For example, double-hung windows are difficult to manage if you have to reach over a sink to get to them. Crank-open casements work more easily in this situation. Lastly, choose windows with a trim style that coordinates with the style of the room.

A SMALL DETAIL
(BELOW) A simple detail like this curved wooden valance above the sink window alters the look of a window quickly. Here it enhances the country theme and reduces harsh afternoon sunlight.

storage

Imagine this—a kitchen where utensils don't live in layers and aren't a long walk from where you need them, where you pull out one pot without putting six back, where everything fits in a designated place, and you know where the soufflé pan is. Kitchens pose storage problems because so many things are kept in them. Plan to contain them from the start so finding them is a breeze.

storage styles

OPEN, EASY ACCESS (BELOW) Open
storage, such as these undercounter
shelves, makes finding the right cooking
utensil easy. Open storage also puts
items on display and requires a certain
amount of organization to keep things
from looking cluttered.

HOW YOU SEE IT. Storage style describes whether a storage unit keeps things visible or under wraps and where it's located. None of the categories listed below are mutually exclusive. Combine one with another to make your kitchen storage flexible and effective.

Open storage keeps items organized but visible. It's for things you need easy access to plus items you enjoy seeing. Almost any horizontal surface from countertops and shelves to glass-front doors and hooks creates open storage.

Closed storage keeps things hidden. This is where unsightly clutter goes—and with the right storage accessories it won't be cluttered anymore. Enclosures with doors, drawers, and lids such as pantries, freestanding units, cabinets, and bins create closed storage.

Convenient storage is storage that's close at hand for things you need regularly. It can be open or closed.

Remote storage keeps things in an area somewhere besides where you use them. This is where the extra rolls of paper towels and seasonal tableware go. Large pantries, the top shelves of tall wall cabinets, and hutches make good choices for remote storage.

Storage styles are about more than containing items. They indicate a personality preference in how you store things. For example, if you won't use something unless you see it, select mostly open storage structures. On the other hand, closed storage might suit you better if you feel distracted by having items in plain sight.

RACK 'EM UP (ABOVE) A pot rack located over an island puts utensils in plain sight and within easy reach. A pot rack is also a fantastic way to show off stylish cookware.

COLOR COORDINATED (ABOVE) Open shelving provides both storage and design opportunities, as this neatly arranged collection of dishware shows. Frequently used items are kept within easy reach and less-used items are stored on top.

ALL-IN-ONE UNIT
(LEFT) An island is a jack-of-all-trades unit. This one offers workspace, display shelves, and utensil storage all wrapped up in the same package.

BASKET BINS (ABOVE) Baskets make a nice alternative to drawers for storing vegetables and other kitchen items. They slide easily out of open shelving.

OPEN AND SHUT (BELOW LEFT AND RIGHT) An appliance garage keeps countertops uncluttered. This one hides appliances behind a tambour door that opens and closes easily. It also includes outlets so appliances can be used right in place.

 CLOSE BY (ABOVE) Located right outside the main kitchen, this walk-in pantry includes a wine rack.

INDEPENDENT DOORS (RIGHT) A carefully designed pantry includes multiple door units independently hinged to view all sections at the same time. Everything tucks together neatly when the unit is closed.

REACH IN (RIGHT) In a kitchen without the floor space for a walk-in pantry, a wall closet provides extra storage. Cabinet doors coordinate the pantry with the kitchen, but because it's recessed into the wall it saves valuable floor space.

pantries

BE PREPARED. Pantries help make good meals, but not merely because they store foodstuffs. With staple items, dry foods, and canned goods well organized and accessible, a pantry makes it easier to figure out what's for dinner tonight.

SUIT YOUR SPACE. Pantries come in an abundance of sizes and configurations. Access and potential for organization are the keys. Pullouts make access convenient and keep items visible so you remember to use them before their expiration dates.

Include tall and wide shelves for bulky items. Shallow shelves less than 16 inches deep make it easier to find items. Pullouts enable you to keep bulky items in the back but still accessible.

Locate the pantry near a countertop so you can park grocery bags close by while restocking. Group similar foods together—canned goods in one section, baking goods in another, pasta and grains in another. Arrange foods in primary and secondary groups. Place primary foods at eye level; stow secondary foods above and below. Paper goods go on the bottom.

A SHORT WALK (RIGHT) Spacious and well organized—and close to the garage—this walk-in pantry makes unpacking and storing groceries a snap.

SEPARATE PIECES
(ABOVE) Two bins
make trash collection
easier and are a boon
for recycling items
that require different
containers.

TWICE AS EASY (RIGHT)
Splitting the storage space
between shelving and the back
of the door makes everything
easier to get at.

**TOUGH AND
FLEXIBLE** (RIGHT)
Adjustable wire racks
in this pullout drawer
accommodate a wide
variety of sizes.

cabinet helpers

A LOOK INSIDE. When you shop for cabinets, you may be surprised at the assortment of accessory options. Of course, the lazy Susan in the corner continues to be a staple storage accessory, but a lot—including the lazy Susan— has changed.

INNOVATIONS. Traditional two-tray lazy Susans still exist, but independently revolving trays greatly improve your access. Units with high sides prevent items from falling off the shelves as you rotate the unit.

A host of swing-out shelves makes small items easy to reach. Touch-and-release drawers in the toe-kicks are designed to stow long, flat items. Vertical racks are handy for keeping cutting boards and baking trays organized and accessible. Drawer inserts are still available to separate utensils, and larger inserts keep stacked plates from chipping. Keep your knives sharp with a knife block or a knife rack in the drawer—some feature a slide-out cutting board on top. And store your pots and pans in a heavy-duty base cabinet pullout tray that's strong enough to carry the weight and extend fully so you can see what's in the back.

HEAVY-DUTY HELP (ABOVE) Large pull-out drawers with heavy-duty glides provide full access to what's inside.

SPIN AROUND (ABOVE) Storing heavy pots and pans on a lazy Susan is possible thanks to sturdy construction. Independently rotating shelves make it easier to access items, and high sides ensure things won't fall off when the shelves are rotated quickly.

STAYING SHARP (ABOVE) A knife block made for a shallow drawer keeps cutting gear sharp. A cork bottom prevents items from sliding around.

customizing **options**

When it comes to storage accessories, manufacturers have left no surface unturned.

Heavy-duty stainless-steel racks may be located inside doors, tucked in drawers, and installed as pullout trays. Plastic-coated racks are less substantial but will hold smaller items easily. Many of these coated racks and baskets are made for installation under existing shelves or on the back of doors, offering you a chance to customize some of your storage solutions.

FOR ODD SIZES
These vertical racks are tall enough to store large casserole dishes, baking trays, and cutting boards.

contact
information

The Home Depot® offers kitchen products and materials from major manufacturers either in stock or through special order. This extensive inventory offers you a comprehensive and varied selection that will ensure a kitchen that truly reflects your style while enabling you to stick to your budget. Because The Home Depot constantly updates its inventory to bring you innovative products and materials, the best source of information on what is currently available can be obtained from The Home Depot associates at your local store or online at www.homedepot.com.

Contacting Meredith Corporation

To order this and other Meredith Corporation books call 800/678-8091. For further information about the information contained in this book, please contact the manufacturers listed or contact Meredith by e-mail at hi123@mdp.com or by phone at 800/678-2093.

Contacting the Home Depot

For general information about product availability contact your local Home Depot or visit The Home Depot website at www.homedepot.com.

Amerock
800/435-6959
www.amerock.com

Catskill Craftsmen
607/652-7321
www.catskillcraftsmen.com

KraftMaid Cabinetry
888/562-7744
www.kraftmaid.com

Thomasville Cabinetry
800/756-6497
www.thomasvillecabinetry.com

Vinotemp
800/777-8466
www.vinotemp.com

Countertops & Backsplashes

Broan-Nuton
888/336-3948
www.nutone.com

Cambria Oxford
866/226-2742
www.cambriausa.com

DuPont Corian
www.corian.com

Silestone by Cosentino
800/291-1311
www.silestoneusa.com

Wilsonart
www.wilsonart.com

Appliances

Cuisinart
800/726-0190
www.cuisinart.com

GE
800/626-2005
www.geappliances.com

Hamilton Beach
800/851-8900
www.hamiltonbeach.com

Jenn-Air
800/536-6247
www.jennair.com

Kitchen Aid
800/541-6390
www.kitchenaid.com

LG
800/243-0000
http://us.lge.com

Maytag Corporation
www.maytag.com

Cabinetry & Hardware

American Woodmark
540/665-9100
www.woodmark-homedepot.com

Flooring

American Marazzi
972/226-0110
www.americanmarazzi.com

Daltile
800/933-8453
www.daltile.com

Pergo
800/337-3746
www.pergo.com

Tarkett
www.tarkett-floors.com/us/

Lighting & Ceiling Fans

Hampton Bay
www.homedepot.com

Progress Lighting
864/599-6000
www.progresslighting.com

Paint

Behr
www.behr.com

Plumbing & Fixtures

American Standard
800/442-1902
www.americanstandard.com

DuPont
www.dupont.com

Grohe America, Inc.
630/582-7711
www.groheamerica.com

International Thermocast Corp.
678/445-2022
www.thermocastsinks.com

Kohler Co.
800/456-4537
www.kohler.com

Moen
800/289-6636
www.moen.com

Price Pfister
800/732-8238
www.pricepfister.com

resources

Listed on the following pages are the names and manufacturers of the products from the six kitchens designed and constructed exclusively from items available from The Home Depot® and that are featured in the first chapter of this book. To determine whether an item shown in the book is still available from The Home Depot contact your local store if the item is listed in the resource section. If it is not listed you will often be able to find an equivalent product within The Home Depot's extensive inventory that is newly improved by the manufacturer.

Colors
Please be aware that paint colors shown in the book may look different on your wall because of the printing process used in this book. If you see a color you like, show it to a Home Depot associate in the paint department, and he or she will custom-tint paint to match it as closely as possible. Buy samples of paint in small quantities and test areas so that you can see the result prior to spending time and money to paint the entire room. Changes in lighting affect colors, which, for instance, can seem remarkably different under artificial light and natural light. Also, consult everyone who will be living with the color. Paint a test area and live with it under different lighting conditions for at least 24 hours to make sure it is right for you.

Pages 8–11

Cabinets: Thomasville Maple Raleigh in Amaretto Crème

Hardware: Thomasville Retro handle pull in matte black; Thomasville Modernistic knob in matte black

Countertop: Silestone Leather Finish Amarillo Palmira

Sink: Kohler Alcott undercounter, K-6753 5U

Faucet: Price Pfister Marielle four-hole single-handle in oil rubbed bronze, 26-4NZZ

Flooring: Daltile Ridgeview ceramic tile

Pages 8–11 (continued)

Lighting: Hampton Bay swag pendant in brushed nickel and etched opal, B 449-404

Wall Paint: Behr flat in Torchlight, 290B-5

Refrigerator: GE Profile stainless-steel 36" side-by-side with dispenser, PSS26MSRSS

Range: GE Profile stainless-steel 30" slide-in electric, JS905SKSS

Range Hood: GE Profile stainless-steel 30" high-performance, JV636HSS

Microwave: GE Profile stainless-steel countertop, JE2160SF

Dishwasher: GE Profile stainless-steel built-in, PDW7880JSS

Pages 12–15

Cabinets: Thomasville Saxony Maple Coffee

Hardware: Thomasville Modernistic pull in satin nickel, M570

Countertop: DuPont Corian Rice Paper

Sink: DuPont Corian integrated

Faucet: Moen Aberdeen stainless-steel one-handle, 7590SL

Flooring: Tarkett Engineered Maple in mahogany glaze, 600-21287 782-038

Lighting: Progress one-light mini pendant, P5070-09

Wall Paint: Behr flat in Rejuvenate, 410E-3

Refrigerator: Maytag ICE20 stainless-steel 36" French door bottom freezer, MFI2568A

Cooktop: Maytag black 36" gas, MGC6536B

Oven: Jenn-Air stainless-steel 30" double electric wall, JJW9430DDS

Microwave: Maytag stainless-steel countertop, UMC5200A

Dishwasher: Maytag JetClean II stainless-steel tall-tub built-in, MDB8751A

Pages 16–19

Cabinets: Kraftmaid Birch Somersworth in Honey Spice and Cabernet

Hardware: Kraftmaid pull, 7026; Kraftmaid knob, 7025

Countertop: Cambria Oxford

Sink: Kohler Lakefield 33×22" cast-iron undercounter with cutting board in black, K-5877-4U

Faucet: Kohler Antique four-hole installation in brushed bronze, K-171-BV

Flooring: Pergo planked laminate in Presto Cherry, PH 4584

Wall Paint: Behr flat in Asparagus, 4100-4

Refrigerator: LG side-by-side smooth in black, LRSC2694OSB

Range: GE Profile 30" freestanding dual fuel in black, J2B912BEKBB

Microwave: GE Profile Spacemaker XL 1800 in black, JVM1870BF

Dishwasher: LG tall-tub stainless interior in black, LDF7810BB

Trash Compactor: GE Profile 15" built-in in black, GCG1520FBB

Pages 20–23

Cabinets: American Woodmark Maple Townsend in Honey and Mocha Glaze

Hardware: American Woodmark square-forged knob, 3222F

Countertop: Wilsonart laminate in Majestic Topaz

Sink: Kohler Staccato stainless 33×22" double-bowl, K-3369-4

Faucet: Kohler Forte single-control with sidespray and level handle in brushed chrome, K-10412-G

Flooring: American Marazzi Pacific Cabos, UD11CA

Lighting: Hampton Bay Imperial Jade Collection natural jade stone/art glass, HD345387

Wall Paint: Behr flat in Earth Tone, 230F-6

Refrigerator: GE Energy Star stainless-steel 36" side-by-side, DSS25KSRSS

Range: GE Adora stainless-steel 30" freestanding electric, JBP83SKSS

Microwave: GE Adora stainless steel, HDM1853SJ

Dishwasher: GE Adora stainless-steel built-in, GHDA656L

Pages 28–29

Cabinets: Kraftmaid Cherry Piermont in Ginger Glaze

Hardware: Kraftmaid brushed chrome knob, 506

Countertops: Beveled granite in English Brown

Sink: Kohler stainless undertone double bowl, K3356

Faucet: Kohler Avatar single-control pullout in brushed nickel with polished nickel accents, B-6352

Flooring: Daltile continental slate in Egyptian Beige

Lighting: Progress Avalon pendant in brushed nickel, P4070-09 P5068-09

Wall Paint: Behr Satin Classic in Taupe, 290 E-30

Refrigerator: GE Monogram stainless-steel 48" built-in side-by-side with dispenser, ZISS48DRSS

Cooktop: GE Monogram 30" ribbon digital electric in black, ZEU30RBFBB

Oven 1: GE Monogram stainless-steel built-in single-wall electric, ZET938SFSS

Oven 2: GE Monogram Advantium stainless-steel built-in wall, ZCS2001FSS

Range hood: GE Monogram stainless-steel 36" Slide-Out hood, ZV800SJSS

Warming Drawer: GE Monogram stainless-steel 30", ZTD910SFSS

Microwave: GE Monogram stainless steel, ZEM910SFSS

Dishwasher: GE Monogram stainless-steel fully integrated, ZBD0710KSS

Bar Fridge: GE Monogram stainless steel, ZIBS240PSS

Pages 36–37

Cabinets: KraftMaid Maple Orchard Park in Vanilla Bean and Ginger Glaze

Hardware: KraftMaid matte nickel pull, 7033

Countertop: DuPont Corian in Canyon

Island Countertop: DuPont Corian in Ruby

Sink: Kohler Deerfield Smart Divide in Thunder Grey, K-5838-7U

Faucet: Kohler Fairfax single-control pull-out in brushed nickel, K-12177-BN

Flooring: Tarkett Contours sheet vinyl, 59013

Lighting: Hampton Bay pendant in brushed nickel and glass, 379-895

Wall Paint: Behr flat in Dolphin Fin, 790C-3

Refrigerator: GE Profile stainless-steel bottom freezer drawer, PDS22BSRSS

Cooktops: GE Profile 30" downdraft electric in black, JP989BKBB; GE Profile 30" built-in gas in black/stainless steel, JGP940SEKSS

Oven: GE Profile stainles-steel 30" built-in convection, JT915SKSS

Range hood: GE Profile stainless-steel 30" designer hood, JV936DSS

Microwave: GE Profile stainless-steel countertop, JE2160SF

Dishwasher: GE Profile stainless interior built-in with hidden controls, PDW9280LSS

index

a-b

t-z